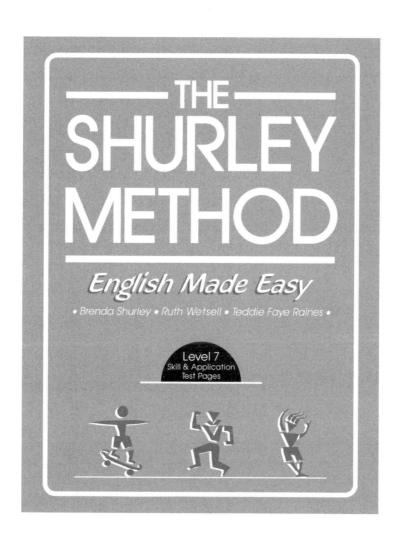

Level 7
Skill & Application Test Pages

SHURLEY INSTRUCTIONAL MATERIALS, INC., CABOT, ARKANSAS

06-21
Shurley English Homeschooling
Level 7 Skill and Application Test Pages
First Edition
ISBN 10: 1-881940-52-7
ISBN 13: 978-1-881940-52-4

Copyright © 1995 by Shurley Instructional Materials, Inc.
No part of this book may be reproduced or transmitted in any form or by any means,
electronic or mechanical, including photocopying, recording, or by any information storage
or retrieval system, without written permission from the Publisher.

Printed in the United States of America by LSC Communications, Owensville, MO.

For additional information or to place an order, write to: Shurley Instructional Materials, Inc.
366 SIM Drive
Cabot, AR 72023

1 2 3 4   21 16 13 95

Level 7 Skill and Application Test Workbook

CHAPTER 1 LESSON 1 PRETEST
(Student Page 1)

Exercise 1: Identify the part of speech or the sentence job of each word. Write the abbreviation above the word.

1. _____ Several plump robins searched diligently for juicy worms in my back yard.

2. _____ For my birthday my generous parents gave me the most important item on my list.

3. _____ Quickly, Jocelyn and her little brother led the five horses into the barn.

4. _____ Four very excited fans were irate after the referee's call!

5. _____ Can that history teacher make this class interesting to his students?

6. _____ My two cousins in El Paso are students at Coronado High School.

7. _____ After an exciting election, John Conner named Sarah Warren chairman of the committee.

Exercise 2: Identify each pronoun as indefinite or personal (**I, P**) and as singular or plural (**S, P**). Underline your choices.

8. we   (I or P) (S or P)   10. everybody (I or P) (S or P)   12. she   (I or P) (S or P)   14. both (I or P) (S or P)
9. each (I or P) (S or P)   11. they   (I or P) (S or P)   13. either (I or P) (S or P)   15. it   (I or P) (S or P)

Exercise 3: Identify each verb as regular or irregular and put **R** or **I** in the blank. Then, write the past tense form.

16. cook _____ _____   17. swim _____ _____   18. break _____ _____

Exercise 4: Fill in the helping verb chart and name the four principal parts of a verb.

19. Write the names of the four principal parts:

Future Tense	Present Perfect		Past Perfect	Future Perfect	Progressive Form		Emphatic Form	
2 verbs	Singular-1	Plural-1	1 verb	3 verbs	Singular -5	Plural - 4	Singular-2	Plural-2

Exercise 5: Correct the errors in the following paragraph. Replace words underlined once with a synonym and words underlined twice with an antonym. Use this editing guide: **Capitals: 27 Homonyms: 6 End Marks: 7 Commas: 4 Semicolons: 1 Subject-Verb Agreement: 4 Apostrophes: 2 Synonym: 3 Antonym: 1 Spelling: 2**

during march my whole family enjoy watching the n c a a division 1 national mens basketball tournament we each <u>choose</u> the too teams we think will make the finals susan and dad <u>always</u> picks u c l a as one of there teams last year some of the games was in kansas city kansas which is near our home sense the games was so close we went two one session and saw for <u>excellent</u> games my <u>dream</u> is to play collage basketball however i am to short i guess ill just have to consintrate on growing

Student Pretest Response Sheet

Write at least a paragraph explaining the benefits of having good English skills.

CHAPTER 1 LESSON 1

Study Skills

Good management skills come from good organizational skills, and organizational skills are the foundation for good study skills. You must learn to manage your time, your materials, and your work environment. Good study skills do not just happen. It takes time, determination, and practicing certain guidelines to get organized. The Study Skills chapter will concentrate on the guidelines you need for success in developing good study habits. Follow them carefully until they become habits that will help you for a lifetime.

Everyone has the same twenty-four hours, but everyone does not use his/her twenty-four hours in the same way. In order to get the most for your time, it is important to set goals. Goals will keep you pointed in the direction you want to go, will focus your time, and will keep you on track. With a list of goals, you can check your progress. Long-term goals are what you want to accomplish in your life, your education, and your career. Short-term goals will help you plan things to do over the next school year, and guidelines will give you specific things to do each day to help you achieve your goals. Write down two long term goals and three short-term goals. Discuss these goals with your teacher, counselor, or parents. You can add more as you think of them. Take time to evaluate your goals at the end of every month to see if there are any adjustments you wish to make. Goals change as your needs change and as your abilities grow.

One of the first steps in good organization is learning how to make and follow a daily schedule or routine. Below is a set of guidelines to help you establish a daily schedule to follow at home and school. These guidelines will be one of the keys to your being successful in school with the least amount of wasted effort.

Beginning Setup Plan for School
You should use this plan to keep things in order!

1. Have separate color-coded pocket folders for each subject.
2. Put unfinished work in the left-hand side and finished work in the right-hand side of each subject folder.
3. Put notes to study, graded tests, and study guides in the brads so you will have them to study for nine weeks or semester tests.
4. Have a trash folder to put all paper to be thrown away. If it doesn't belong in a folder, throw it away!
5. Have a paper folder to store extra clean sheets of paper. Keep it full at all times.
6. Have an assignment folder to be reviewed every day. (This is a very important folder. It must go home every night!)

Do these things and put them in your assignment folder:
   A. Keep a monthly calendar of homework assignments, test dates, report-due dates, project-due dates, meeting times, after-school activities, dates and times, review dates, etc.
   B. Keep a grade sheet to record the grades received in each class. (You might also consider keeping your grades on the inside cover of each subject folder. However you keep your grades, just remember to keep up with them accurately, even if you have to ask for your grades at the end of every week. Your grades are your business, so keep up with them!)
   C. Make a list every day of the things you want to do so that you can keep track of what you finish and what you do not finish. Move the unfinished items to your new list the next day. (Yes, making this list takes some time, but it's your road map to success. You will always know at a glance what you set out to accomplish and what still needs to be done.)

7. Organize your locker, get rid of unnecessary papers, keep locker trips to a minimum. (There should be **no loose papers** in your locker!)
8. Keep all necessary school supplies in a handy, heavy-duty plastic bag or a pencil bag.

CHAPTER 1 LESSON 1

Study Plan for School
You should check this plan every day!

1. Attend class regularly after eating breakfast to start your day.
2. Schoolwork is your job -- make it an important part of your daily life.
3. Develop the "I'm-willing-to-do-what-it-takes-to-get-the-job-done" attitude.
4. Work with your teachers and parents to correct any attitudes or habits that keep you from learning.
5. Make the effort to listen, ask questions if you don't understand, and answer questions if asked.
6. Write it down! Write it down! Write it down! Make taking notes in class a habit. Then, put them in the correct folder.
7. Ask about make-up work and turn it in on time.
8. Turn your daily assignments in on time.
9. Check your assignment folder every day. Know what is on your calendar. Remember to record everything on your calendar so you won't get behind!
10. Concentrate on the job at hand. If you don't waste time, you will have a chance to finish your work. Keep your eyes on your work and keep your pencil moving. Don't give yourself a chance to stop working by breaking your concentration. Every time your eyes leave your paper to look around, you lose working time.
11. Do what is important first! Assignments that are due first should be completed first.
12. Think before you leave school! Check your assignment folder and decide what you need to take home. Put books and folders you will need in a book bag so you won't forget them.

Study Plan for Home
Stick to this plan every evening!

1. Schedule a time to study. Think about your family's routine and decide on a good study time. Stick to your schedule.
2. Study where you can concentrate. Sorry! No TV or telephone while you study! (Get your studying job finished and then watch TV or talk on the telephone, if you must. Remember, TV does not get you ahead in life--Education will!)
3. Make a personal decision to concentrate 100 percent on completing your homework assignments. You will get more accomplished in less time with 100 percent concentration than if you give 25 percent of your concentration for a longer period of time.
4. Check your assignment folder every day. Get control of your life!
5. Have a special place to keep homework. When your homework is finished, put it in your bookbag right then, and you will always have it ready to take to school, no matter how hassled your morning is.
6. Use your home study time to get your assignments done or to review for a test. Don't wait until the last minute to study for a test. Study a little every night so that you won't overload the night before. (And, of course, you'll probably have company the night before the big test! That's why you don't wait until the last minute to study – take charge!)
7. If possible, set a weekly meeting time to discuss your progress with your parents. If it is not possible, meet with yourself. You need to discuss your progress and problems. See which study skill you did not follow. Figure out what to do to "fix" them, and try again! You'll get better with practice.
8. You are old enough to help yourself! Remember, school is your business, your job, and your responsibility.

CHAPTER 1 LESSON 1
Student Progress Chart

School is your job. Make it your business to know your progress. The progress chart below is designed for you to record and graph your grades in each subject so you can see your progress. You will know from day to day how you are doing in every subject. You will see from your progress chart if you need to do extra studying in a particular subject.

Write the month and each day's date in the appropriate boxes. Write your percentage grade in the box beside the corresponding letter grade. Your chart will record up to twenty grades.

Student Progress Chart
You should chart your grades with colored pencils.

Month:																					
Day:																					
English	1	2	3	4	5	6	7	8	9	10	11	12	13	14	15	16	17	18	19	20	Average
A																					
B																					
C																					
D																					
F																					
Day:																					
Math	1	2	3	4	5	6	7	8	9	10	11	12	13	14	15	16	17	18	19	20	Average
A																					
B																					
C																					
D																					
F																					
Day:																					
Science	1	2	3	4	5	6	7	8	9	10	11	12	13	14	15	16	17	18	19	20	Average
A																					
B																					
C																					
D																					
F																					
Day:																					
History	1	2	3	4	5	6	7	8	9	10	11	12	13	14	15	16	17	18	19	20	Average
A																					
B																					
C																					
D																					
F																					

Other:

CHAPTER 1 LESSON 1

The first pages of this book discuss some of the ways for you to manage your time, your materials, and your work environment by making and following a daily schedule, or routine. Now, you will use the *Daily Lesson Record* below to record your assignments and grades. This daily lesson record will help you remember what you do in class, when assignments or projects are due, and what weekly grades you make in each subject.

Daily Lesson Record					
Teacher:		Class:	Period:	For the Week of:	
Class Activity	Monday	Tuesday	Wednesday	Thursday	Friday
Book Page Nos.					
Class Worksheet					
Test					
Homework					
Project					
Project Due Date					
Library, Film, Etc.					
Grades Made					
Work Not Turned In					
Incomplete Work					

Daily Lesson Record					
Teacher:		Class:	Period:	For the Week of:	
Class Activity	Monday	Tuesday	Wednesday	Thursday	Friday
Book Page Nos.					
Class Worksheet					
Test					
Homework					
Project					
Project Due Date					
Library, Film, Etc.					
Grades Made					
Work Not Turned In					
Incomplete Work					

CHAPTER 1 LESSON 2 SKILL TEST
(Student Page 7)

Exercise 1: Write **a** or **an** in the blanks.

1. We heard _____ amazing story!
2. We heard _____ story that amazed us!
3. _____ ice fairy was the main character.
4. _____ fairy was the main character.
5. It was _____ exciting evening.
6. They had _____ lovely evening.
7. _____ oriole built _____ outstanding nest.
8. _____ pair of orioles built _____ sturdy nest.

Exercise 2: Identify each pair of words as synonyms **(syn)** or antonyms **(ant)** by putting parentheses ( ) around **syn** or **ant**.

#	Words	syn/ant	#	Words	syn/ant
9.	model, copy	syn ant	15.	sincere, dishonest	syn ant
10.	ancient, modern	syn ant	16.	seize, surrender	syn ant
11.	feeble, frail	syn ant	17.	relish, enjoy	syn ant
12.	deprive, enrich	syn ant	18.	quiver, vibrate	syn ant
13.	robust, strong	syn ant	19.	heterogeneous, unlike	syn ant
14.	taunt, harass	syn ant	20.	brawny, weak	syn ant

Exercise 3: Underline the correct homonym.

21. (Their, There, They're) new car is red.
22. (Its, It's) a great ball game!
23. (Your, You're) free to go.
24. Our guide (lead, led) us to safety.
25. (Their, They're) going with us to the game.
26. This pink (stationary, stationery) is pretty.
27. Place the punch bowl (their, there) on the table.
28. The band was (stationary, stationery) during the song.
29. The high school band marched (fourth, forth) onto the field.
30. Several of the (principals, principles) of management were discussed at our meeting.
31. The cautious marines quietly slipped (threw, through) the enemy lines.
32. Jake used my father's old wrench to repair the (led, lead) pipe.
33. The teacher asked for the (right, write) answer to the essay question.
34. A very talented musical group won (their, there) first trophy yesterday.
35. Dad asked for a (course, coarse) grade of sandpaper at the hardware store.
36. The frightened rabbit stood (stationary, stationery) as the car approached.
37. The starting quarterback (threw, through) a pass for the winning touchdown!
38. The soldiers trained for battle on a grueling obstacle (coarse, course).
39. All of the club members (no, know) the date of their next meeting.

Exercise 4:   Editing Paragraph
Find each error and write the correction above it. Replace words underlined once with a synonym and words underlined twice with an antonym. **Editing Guide: Homonyms: 7 Synonyms: 5 Antonyms: 1 A/An: 1 Misspelled Words: 5 Missing Words: 1**

The kindergardeners had to decide which of the to paths lead back to there knew school. They didn't

no which one to <u>pick</u>. Finaly their principal came too they're rescue. The <u>little</u> boys <u>went</u> meakly back

with principle. He gave them a extra cool glass of <u>water</u> while they sat <u>inside</u> his office and missed

<u>playtime</u>.

CHAPTER 1 LESSON 3 APPLICATION TEST
(Student Page 8)

Exercise 1: Write **a** or **an** in the blanks.

1. We studied about _____ ancient tribe of Indians.
2. We studied about _____ tribe of Indians from South America.
3. Each child enjoyed _____ orange carrot for a snack.
4. The rabbit ate _____ carrot for his lunch.

Exercise 2: Identify each pair of words as synonyms **(syn)** or antonyms **(ant)** by putting parentheses ( ) around **syn** or **ant**.

5. suspect, distrust	syn ant	9. expense, income	syn ant	13. melancholy, gloomy	syn ant
6. foolish, prudent	syn ant	10. quaint, ordinary	syn ant	14. entertain, annoy	syn ant
7. question, doubt	syn ant	11. saw, spied	syn ant	15. costly, worthless	syn ant
8. soothe, pacify	syn ant	12. error, blunder	syn ant	16. hasten, delay	syn ant

Exercise 3: Underline the correct homonym.

17. The racing (course, coarse) was five miles long.
18. The (capital, capitol) of Idaho is Boise.
19. My grandmother wrote her letters on beautiful (stationery, stationary).
20. The (course, coarse) gravel was dumped on the side of the road.
21. The (capital, capitol) building in Arkansas is beautiful.
22. The cat was (stationery, stationary) a moment before she pounced on the mouse.
23. (They're, Their) cousin sent them five tickets to the game.
24. The baby was (to, too) noisy to be taken to the library.
25. The city (counsel, council) met to vote on the water proposal.
26. (Your, You're) allowed to write this report in ink.

Exercise 4:   Editing Paragraph
Find each error and write the correction above it. Replace words underlined once with a synonym and words underlined twice with an antonym. **Editing Guide: Homonyms: 7   Synonyms: 5   Antonyms: 2   A/An: 2   Misspelled Words: 7   Missing Words: 1**

Yesterday I went to my brother's basketball game. First I walked quickly threw an metal detector on my way to the bleachers. I sat on the forth row. The cherleaders lead the large crowd in wild cheers for each team. The principles of each school yelled louder than anyone. The too teams were unevenly matched, and this game ended in a tie. No one was two disapointed, and each team left court amid an thundous applase from there fathful fans.

CHAPTER 1 LESSON 4

What is Journal Writing?

Journal Writing is a written record of your personal thoughts and feelings about things or people that are important to you. Recording your thoughts in a journal is a good way to remember how you felt about what was happening in your life at a particular time. You can record your dreams, memories, feelings, and experiences. You can ask questions and answer some of them. It can be fun to go back later and read what you have written because it can show how you have grown on the inside and changed in different areas of your life. A journal can also be an excellent place to look for future writing topics, creative stories, poems, etc. Writing in a journal is an easy and enjoyable way to practice your writing skills without worrying about a writing grade.

What Do I Write About?

Journals are personal, but sometimes it helps to have ideas to get you started. Remember, in a journal, you do not have to stick to one topic. Write about someone or something in school. Write about what you did last weekend or on vacation. Write about what you hope to do this week or on your next vacation. Write about home, school, friends, enemies, hobbies, special talents (yours or someone else's), present and future hopes and fears. Write about what is wrong in your world and what you would do to "fix" it. Write about the good things and the bad things in your world. If you think about a past event and want to write an opinion about it now, put it in your journal. If you want to give your opinion about a present or future event that could have an impact on your life or the way you see things, put it in your journal. If something bothers you, record it in your journal. If something interests you, record it. If you just want to record something that doesn't seem important at all, write it in your journal. After all, it is your journal!

How Do I Get Started Writing in My Personal Journal?

You need to put a journal-entry heading on the title line of your paper with the day's date. Example:
    Journal Entry for September 3, 20____.
Skip the next line and begin your entry. You might write a paragraph, a whole page, or several pages. Except for the journal-entry title with the date, no particular organizational style is required for journal writing. You decide how best to organize and express your thoughts. Feel free to include sketches, diagrams, lists, etc., if they will help you remember your thoughts about a topic or an event.

You will also need a spiral notebook, a pen,* a quiet place, and at least 5-10 minutes of uninterrupted writing time.

*(Use a pen if possible. Pencils have lead points that break and erasers, both of which slow down your thoughts. Any drawings you might include do not have to be masterpieces--stick figures will do nicely.)

Journal Writing Assignment: Make an entry in your journal. Follow the instructions on journal entries above.

CHAPTER 2 LESSON 2 SKILL TEST
(Student Page 18)

Exercise 1: Classify this sentence.

1. _____ Three dangerous lions raced rapidly away!

Exercise 2: Use the Editing Guide below each sentence to know how many capitalization and punctuation errors to correct. Write the capitalization corrections and rule numbers above each word. Write the punctuation corrections and rule numbers below each word. Use the capitalization and punctuation rule pages to get the correct rule numbers.

1. no john you cant hike up temple mountain and camp at silver lake with james billy and larry

   Editing Guide: Capitals: 9   Commas: 4   Apostrophes: 1   End Marks: 1

2. aunt sue my moms sister visited hoover dam in nevada on march 31 1993 during easter vacation

   Editing Guide: Capitals: 7   Commas: 4   Apostrophes: 1   End Marks: 1

3. last july i went to an italian restaurant with joe my australian friend and ordered a caesar salad

   Editing Guide: Capitals: 7   Commas: 2   End Marks: 1

Exercise 3:   **Editing Paragraph**
Find each error and correct it. Write the capitalization corrections above each word. Write the punctuation corrections below each word. Use the capitalization and punctuation rule pages to review the rules. (Do not write the rule numbers.)
Editing Guide: Capitals: 23   Commas: 9   End Marks: 7

san francisco is a city with lots of personality clanging cable cars carry visitors up and down the

steep hilly and narrow streets tourists wait in lines to take their cars down lombard street the curviest

street in america visitors to the pier can tour a world war II submarine watch the sea lions playing from

the seal rock cafe or enjoy a performance by a street musician the nearby island of alcatraz offers a tour

of the prison that once housed al capone the gangster chinatown known for its pagodas and exotic

shops sits right in the middle of downtown san francisco yes san francisco is an interesting place to see

CHAPTER 2 LESSON 3 APPLICATION TEST
(Student Page 19)

Exercise 1: Classify each sentence.

1. _____ A dangerous copperhead slithered silently nearby!

2. _____ The very funny comedian laughed quite often.

3. _____ The five weary hikers trudged home slowly yesterday.

Exercise 2: Write the capitalization corrections and rule numbers above each word. Write the punctuation corrections and rule numbers below each word. Use the Editing Guide to know how many errors to correct.

---

4. linda my uncles brother b j sims has taught history at cleveland high school in copper springs texas since september 5 1985 and is the author of the well-known book called war between the states

Editing Guide: Capitals: 14   Commas: 7   Periods: 2   Apostrophes: 1   Underlining: 1   End Marks: 1

---

5. grandpa rice tina and susan traveled to washington d c to visit bob k sparkman last july mr sparkman took them to see the lincoln memorial and the potomac river they visited mount vernon the home of george washington

Editing Guide: Capitals: 22   Commas: 5   Periods: 4   End Marks: 3

Exercise 3:   Editing Paragraph
Find each error and write the correction above it. Replace words underlined once with a synonym and words underlined twice with an antonym. **Editing Guide: Homonyms: 18   Synonyms: 3   Antonyms: 1   A/An: 1   Misspelled Words: 2   Capitals: 12   End Marks: 8**

jan and jill had fun yesterday they're goverment class went to the <u>new</u> capital building to watch the

general council right laws a tour guide lead there class threw an tunnel too an extra <u>big</u> room where

the counsel met to men were debating the principals of seatbelt safety one man got two excited

and through his stationary all over the floor the other man charged fourth with glee to pick it up the

principle speaker had to tell the <u>excited</u> men to stop there coarse behavier and to act write jan and jill

<u>saw</u> everything from the forth row of seats

CHAPTER 3 LESSON 2 SKILL TEST
(Student Page 26)

Exercise 1: Match the definitions. Write the correct letter beside each numbered concept.

_____ 1. noun	A. verb, adjective, or adverb
_____ 2. subject noun question (person)	B. who
_____ 3. subject noun question (thing)	C. what is being said about
_____ 4. verb question	D. person, place, thing
_____ 5. adverb modifies	E. what
_____ 6. adjective modifies	F. complete predicate
_____ 7. article adjective can be called	G. shows strong feeling
_____ 8. punctuation for declarative	H. inverted order
_____ 9. adverb that comes right before the verb	I. noun or pronoun
_____ 10. exclamatory sentence	J. exclamation point
_____ 11. punctuation for exclamatory sentence	K. adverb exception
_____ 12. all the predicate parts	L. period
_____ 13. all the subject parts	M. noun marker
_____ 14. sentence with predicate words in the complete subject	N. verb
_____ 15. word that usually starts the complete predicate	O. complete subject

Exercise 2: Fill in the blank: Write the answer for each question.

16. What is the Question and Answer Flow for an exclamatory sentence? _____
17. What word tells what the subject does? _____
18. What are the three article adjectives? _____
19. What are all the parts in the predicate of a sentence called? _____
20. What are the adjective questions? _____
21. Name two noun jobs. _____

Exercise 3: Classify each sentence and then complete the noun job table.

22. _____ The spoiled Doberman begs for dog biscuits during the dinner meal.

List the Noun Used	List the Noun Job	Singular or Plural	Common or Proper
23.	24.	25.	26.
27.	28.	29.	30.
31.	32.	33.	34.

35. _____ Aunt Sara stood silently by the shore of Windy Lake.

List the Noun Used	List the Noun Job	Singular or Plural	Common or Proper
36.	37.	38.	39.
40.	41.	42.	43.
44.	45.	46.	47.

CHAPTER 3 LESSON 3 APPLICATION TEST
(Student Page 27)

Exercise 1: Classify each sentence.

1. _____ Yesterday the confident debater spoke clearly to the audience during the competition.

2. _____ The famous dancers bowed gracefully to Sara from the dance floor.

3. _____ During the summer months vegetables grow in abundance in the valleys of California.

Directions: Complete the noun job table. Use Sentence 3.

List the Noun Used	List the Noun Job	Singular or Plural	Common or Proper
4.	5.	6.	7.
8.	9.	10.	11.
12.	13.	14.	15.
16.	17.	18.	19.
20.	21.	22.	23.

Exercise 2: Match the definitions. Write the correct letter or letters beside each numbered concept.

_____ 24. all the predicate parts
_____ 25. all the subject parts
_____ 26. adjective questions
_____ 27. adverb questions
_____ 28. declarative sentence
_____ 29. predicate words in the subject
_____ 30. simple predicate
_____ 31. simple subject
_____ 32. words with the same meaning
_____ 33. words opposite in meaning
_____ 34. five parts of a sentence
_____ 35. words pronounced the same but are different in meaning

A. subject noun
B. subject
C. homonyms
D. what kind
E. statement
F. complete predicate
G. how
H. inverted order
I. complete subject
J. noun
K. antonyms
L. synonyms

M. verb
N. verb
O. preposition
P. adverb
Q. sense
R. which one
S. adjective
T. capital letter
U. where
V. end mark
W. when
X. how many

Exercise 3: Write a prepositional phrase with two modifiers.

36. _____

Exercise 4:   Editing Paragraph
Find each error and write the correction above it. Replace words underlined once with a synonym. **Editing Guide:**
Homonyms: 4 Synonyms: 4 A/An: 1 Misspelled Words: 2 Capitals: 20 Commas: 2 Periods: 3 End Marks: 5
Underlining: 1 Apostrophes: 1

all students at conway high school must read a tale of two cities by charles dickens in there high school english class the english teacher mr c r green <u>shows</u> his class how too right a <u>good</u> report on this book then the principle <u>chooses</u> the best report the winner will repersent the school in an national compition its <u>good</u> fun

CHAPTER 4 LESSON 2 SKILL TEST
(Student Page 34)

Subject-Verb Agreement Rule Box
1. A singular subject must use a singular verb or a singular verb form: *is, was, has, does,* or verbs ending with **s** or **es**.
2. A plural subject must use a plural verb or a plural verb form: *are, were, do, have,* or verbs without **s** or **es** endings. (A plural verb form without **s** or **es** endings is called a *plain form*).
3. The subject **YOU** is considered plural. Always use a plural verb or a plural verb form (see the plural verb list above).

Exercise 1: Underline the subject noun once and the correct verb twice. Put the verb rule number (**1, 2, 3**) in the blank.

_____ 1. Cody and Mike (trade, trades) baseball cards often.
_____ 2. My mountain bike (race, races) better than anyone else's!
_____ 3. Those cowboys (is, are) practicing for the rodeo tonight.
_____ 4. One row of seats (is, are) still completely vacant.
_____ 5. Five stamps from the post office (was, were) placed on the letters.
_____ 6. You (was, were) playing your trumpet too loudly.
_____ 7. The icicles on our roof (has, have) melted this morning.
_____ 8. My new shoes (has, have) dark brown shoelaces.
_____ 9. The leaves of the bush (does, do) not change colors in the fall.
_____ 10. You (does, do) not need to use a straw in your drink.
_____ 11. Spotted owls (live, lives) in the forests of Oregon and California.
_____ 12. You (win, wins) a gold medal in the skating competition.
_____ 13. Two sacks of money (was, were) found in the parking lot!
_____ 14. Joe and John (is, are) floating in a canoe on the river this weekend.
_____ 15. You (was, were) late for your appointment two days in a row.

Exercise 2: Answer the questions below.

16. Name the seven subject pronouns.

17. Name the understood subject pronoun.

18. How do you label and mark the understood subject pronoun?

19. What is an imperative sentence?

20. What is the Question and Answer Flow for an imperative sentence?

21. Name the seven object pronouns.

Exercise 3:   Editing Paragraph
Underline each verb that has an error in subject-verb agreement. Then, write the correction above it. Use the Editing Guide to know how many errors to correct. **Editing Guide: Subject-Verb Agreement: 7**

Our family have a hard time teaching my dad to stay out of the refrigerator at night. He do not know we is watching him sneak late night snacks. Mom try to sleep with one eye open so she can catch him getting up. Our dog, Arf, help Mom keep an eye on Dad. Arf growl at Dad when he try to leave the bedroom.

Level 7 Skill and Application Test Workbook

CHAPTER 4 LESSON 3 APPLICATION TEST
(Student Page 35)

Exercise 1: Classify each sentence.

1. _____ Yesterday he spoke to the students about the location of ancient tribes of Indians.

2. _____ Look at the world map on the south wall in the public library.

3. _____ Gigantic trees stand on a carpet of green grass at the edge of the thick forest.

Directions: Complete the noun job table. Use Sentence 3.

List the Noun Used	List the Noun Job	Singular or Plural	Common or Proper
4.	5.	6.	7.
8.	9.	10.	11.
12.	13.	14.	15.
16.	17.	18.	19.
20.	21.	22.	23.

Subject-Verb Agreement Rule Box
1. A singular subject must use a singular verb or a singular verb form: *is, was, has, does,* or verbs ending with **s** or **es**.
2. A plural subject must use a plural verb or a plural verb form: *are, were, do, have,* or verbs without **s** or **es** endings. (A plural verb form without **s** or **es** endings is called a *plain form*).
3. The subject **YOU** is considered plural. Always use a plural verb or a plural verb form (see the plural verb list above).

Exercise 2: Underline the subject noun once and the correct verb twice. Put the verb rule number (**1, 2, 3**) in the blank.

_____ 24. Cindy (wash, washes) all the dirty clothes on Monday.

_____ 25. Kelly and Steven (ride, rides) their new bikes everywhere!

_____ 26. Those ducks (is, are) eating our grass seed.

_____ 27. The book about dolphins (is, are) on the book shelf.

_____ 28. Robert and Tommy (was, were) shopping at the bicycle shop.

_____ 29. They (was, were) nervous about their math test.

_____ 30 The band instructor (has, have) several beginning students in his class.

_____ 31. The children (has, have) enough free time to play outside.

_____ 32. She (do, does) eat vegetables for every meal.

_____ 33. Several lamps (do, does) not burn brightly at all.

Exercise 3:   **Editing Paragraph**
Find each error and write the correction. Replace words underlined once with a synonym and words underlined twice with an antonym. Use the Editing Guide to help you. **Editing Guide: Homonyms: 4 Synonyms: 2 Antonyms: 2 A/An: 1 Misspelled Words: 2 Capitals: 6 Apostrophes: 1 Subject-Verb Agreement: 5 End Marks: 6**

several geese lives in the <u>tiny</u> pond in front of our house twice a day they leave the pond and follow there leader up the hill too our neighborhood one goose have an broken foot and walk along behind the others they <u>walk</u> around slowly and patently looking for food and waiting for the <u>hurt</u> one to catch up they honks and fuss if children gets two close its fun watching the geese visit our <u>quiet</u> neighborhood

Level 7 Skill and Application Test Workbook

CHAPTER 5 LESSON 2 SKILL TEST
(Student Page 42)

Subject-Verb Agreement Rules for Special Cases
1. Singular collective nouns (united action, all together) 2. Plural collective nouns (separate actions, one by one) 3. Nouns singular in meaning but plural in form 4. Plural *ics* nouns 5. Singular *ics* nouns 6. Titles or names of countries 7. Words of amount and time 8. Amount or time with plural object of the preposition 9. *And* compound 10. *Or, Nor* compound 11. Inverted sentence

Exercise 1: Underline the subject once. In the *Sp Case* column, write the special case rule number of the subject from the box above. In the *S/P* column, write *S* if the subject is singular or *P* if the subject is plural. Then, underline the verb twice that agrees with the special subject.

Sp Case	S/P	
		1. The band (was, were) playing beautifully.
		2. The band (was, were) running away in all directions.
		3. Either private cars or a chartered bus (is, are) taking us there.
		4. Either a chartered bus or private cars (is, are) taking us there.
		5. The fifteen minutes (seem, seems) more like fifteen hours!
		6. The enthusiastic audience (clap, claps) wildly for the singer.
		7. *The Three Musketeers* (is, are) a book that has been made into a movie.
		8. Neither the chairs nor the tables (has, have) arrived.
		9. Athletics (produce, produces) healthy, fit young people.
		10. Eight weeks never (seem, seems) long enough for our summer vacation.
		11. The mumps (is, are) widespread in our community.
		12. Neither the principal nor the teacher (is, are) able to come to the phone.
		13. The entire group (believe, believes) in hard work.
		14. The class (disagree, disagrees) on a theme for the dance.
		15. Jack and Jill (is, are) going up the hill.
		16. The news (is, are) on a local channel.
		17. The army of ants (march, marches) busily along the sidewalk.
		18. There (is, are) a large area of new homes.
		19. Politics in a business office (is, are) dangerous.
		20. My sister's politics (seem, seems) to change every year.
		21. The jury (was, were) in hot disagreement.
		22. The United Nations (is, are) sending a team to the Middle East.
		23. Twenty pounds of apples (was, were) sent to us.
		24. Our family (spend, spends) time together every Sunday afternoon.
		25. Five tons (is, are) the average weight of most elephants.

Exercise 2: Answer the questions below.

26. Name the seven possessive pronouns.

27. What do possessive pronouns and possessive nouns show?

28. What punctuation mark does a possessive noun always have?

29. What is the question you ask in the Question and Answer Flow to find possessive words?

30. Name the seven subject pronouns.

CHAPTER 5 LESSON 3 APPLICATION TEST
(Student Page 43)

Exercise 1: Classify each sentence.

1. _____ Yesterday the dog's teeth snapped viciously at the intruder's leg!

2. _____ During study hall we reviewed quickly for our big math test.

3. _____ The thieves' fingerprints were on Mr. Bank's desk in his office.

Directions: Complete the noun job table. Use Sentence 3.

List the Noun Used	List the Noun Job	Singular or Plural	Common or Proper
4.	5.	6.	7.
8.	9.	10.	11.
12.	13.	14.	15.
16.	17.	18.	19.
20.	21.	22.	23.

Exercise 2: Underline the subject noun once. In the *S/P* column, write **S** if the subject is singular or **P** if the subject is plural. Underline the correct verb twice to agree with the subject.

S/P	
	24. The whole class (practice, practices) hard every day on its play.
	25. Mathematics (is, are) a required course every year at our school.
	26. Mumps (is, are) sometimes a very painful illness.
	27. *Two Gentlemen of Verona* (is, are) one of Shakespeare's early comedies.
	28. The Netherlands (is, are) a land of plentiful water and beautiful flowers.
	29. One hundred pounds (is, are) the average weight of the young swim team.
	30. Two weeks never (seem, seems) long enough for our vacation.
	31. Neither Jack nor the boys (like, likes) Italian food.
	32. Where (is, are) the box for these ornaments?

Exercise 3: Editing Paragraph
Find each error and write the correction. Replace words underlined once with a synonym. Use the Editing Guide to know how many errors to correct. **Editing Guide: Capitals: 24 Homonyms: 4 Subject-Verb Agreement: 8 Synonyms: 2 Apostrophes: 2 Periods: 3 Misspelled Words: 4 End Marks: 13**

the united states have good doctors for animals doctors for animals is called veternarians i <u>like</u> working for a veterinarian every tuesday i work at dr bensons veterinery clinic dr benson let me feed and exercise the animals usually i takes care of the dogs and cats ben and adam is my favorite dogs their always <u>glad</u> to see me because they no I feed them and let them out of there cages three hours are all i work three-fourths of my job is great i only have one problem dr bensons parrot get on my nerves he talk to mush

CHAPTER 6 LESSON 2 SKILL TEST
(Student Page 49)

Exercise 1: Use the rule box *Making Nouns Possessive* to complete the exercise below. For Test 1, underline each noun to be made possessive and write singular or plural (**S-P**), the rule number, and the possessive form. For Test 2, write each noun as singular possessive and then as plural possessive. For Test 3 and Test 4, rewrite each phrase and use a possessive noun.

Making Nouns Possessive						
Decide if the noun you want to make possessive is singular or plural before you add the apostrophe. Follow these rules.						
1. For a singular noun - add (**'s**) boy's			2. For a plural noun that ends in **s** - add (**'**) boys'		3. For a plural noun that does not end in **s** - add (**'s**) men's	
Test 1				Test 2		
Nouns	S-P	Rule	Possessive Form	Nouns	Singular Poss	Plural Poss
1. eagle wings				16. clock		
2. boots laces				17. scientist		
3. geese feathers				18. child		
4. horse bridle				19. pony		
5. flutes notes				20. mouse		
6. mice trap				21. dish		
7. bus windows				22. baby		
8. glasses rims				23. man		
9. fish tank				24. driver		
10. tomato seeds				25. teacher		
11. oxen hooves				26. coach		
12. tiger stripes				27. Kelly		
13. mirrors frames				28. tooth		
14. game score				29. leaf		
15. ladies shoes				30. crowd		
Test 3				Test 4		
31. the bibs of the babies				35. the bikes of the boys		
32. the ties of the men				36. the bikes of the boy		
33. the pizza of the girls				37. the claws of the bear		
34. the store of Amy				38. the speed of the jets		

Exercise 2: Answer each question below.

39. What part of speech is the word NOT?
40. Write the punctuation for an interrogative sentence.
41. What punctuation is used for possessive nouns?
42. What are the two jobs of the possessive noun?

43. List the 8 *be* verbs.

44. List the 15 other helping verbs.

Exercise 3: Underline all the nouns that need an apostrophe. Write the correct possessive form. **Possessive nouns: 6**

Our schools musical production is coming soon! The choirs songs are beginning to sound wonderful. All the choir members hard work is paying off. The bands music sounds beautiful, too. The bands director is especially pleased with his students performance in practice and in competition.

CHAPTER 6 LESSON 3 APPLICATION TEST
(Student Page 50)

Exercise 1: Classify each sentence.

1. _____ The entry words in a dictionary are arranged in alphabetical order.

2. _____ The buried treasure of Captain Kidd was never found by the sailors.

3. _____ Are the twins going to the fair with you tonight?

Directions: Complete the noun job table. Use Sentence 2.

List the Noun Used	List the Noun Job	Singular or Plural	Common or Proper
4.	5.	6.	7.
8.	9.	10.	11.
12.	13.	14.	15.

Exercise 2: Use the rule box *Making Nouns Possessive* to complete each exercise below. For Test 1, underline each noun to be made possessive and write singular or plural (**S-P**), the rule number, and the possessive form. For Test 2, write each noun as singular possessive and then as plural possessive. For Test 3 and Test 4, rewrite each phrase and use a possessive noun.

Making Nouns Possessive		
Decide if the noun you want to make possessive is singular or plural before you add the apostrophe. Follow these rules.		
1. For a singular noun - add (**'s**) boy's	2. For a plural noun that ends in **s** - add (**'**) boys'	3. For a plural noun that does not end in **s** - add (**'s**) men's

Test 1				Test 2		
Nouns	S-P	Rule	Possessive Form	Nouns	Singular Poss	Plural Poss
16. shirts sleeves				21. party		
17. women voices				22. radio		
18. James room				23. calf		
19. sheep pen				24. ox		
20. pianos keys				25. bus		
Test 3				Test 4		
26. the tails of dogs				30. the spikes of the boot		
27. the traps of the mice				31. the limbs of the trees		
28. house of the Smiths				32. the pages of the book		
29. the hair of Susie				33. the pets of children		

Exercise 3:   Editing Paragraph
Find each error and write the correction. Replace words underlined once with a synonym. Use the Editing Guide to help you. **Editing Guide: Homonyms: 1 Synonyms: 4 Capitals: 21 Subject-Verb Agreement: 4 Misspelled Words: 5 Commas: 8 Apostrophes: 4 Underline: 1 End Marks: 5**

the sluggers our towns little league baseball team travel to omaha nebraska for their <u>big</u> championship tornament on labor day weekend the players baseball shoes is donated by sams shoe store in topeka kansas for this <u>event</u> all the parents is going to the <u>final</u> game on satuday to suport the sluggers there hometown newspaper the kansas sun write <u>big</u> artcles about the girls trip every thusday the team like it

CHAPTER 7 LESSON 2 SKILL TEST
(Student Page 62)

Exercise 1: Write *any*, *no*, or *none* to correctly complete each sentence.

1. Susie couldn't find _____ pencils.
2. Susie could find _____ pencil to do her work.
3. Susie did _____ of the things on the list.
4. Jason hasn't _____ pencils to do his work.
5. Anne had _____ paper plates for the picnic.
6. We could find _____ of the lost coins.

Exercise 2: Underline the negative words in the sentences below. On a sheet of notebook paper, write two ways to correct each double negative.

7. Rhonda hasn't never driven our car.
8. Nick didn't talk to no one on the telephone.
9. Our car wasn't going nowhere with that flat!
10. This shortwave radio isn't doing us no good.
11. I don't have no excuse.
12. We couldn't get nothing out of the burning house.

Exercise 3: Write the different forms and rule numbers for these adjectives or adverbs. For irregular forms write **Irr** in the rule box.

Comparative Rules: Rule 1. -er Rule 2. use **more** with -ly or -ful or awkward words. Rule 3. use **more** for 3 or more syllable words.
Superlative Rules: Rule 1. -est Rule 2. use **most** with -ly or -ful or awkward words. Rule 3. use **most** for 3 or more syllable words.

Simple Adjective/Adverb	Rule	Comparative Form	Rule	Superlative Form
13. sharp	14.	15.	16.	17.
18. smoothly	19.	20.	21.	22.
23. busy	24.	25.	26.	27.
28. fast	29.	30.	31.	32.
33. beautiful	34.	35.	36.	37.
38.	39.	40. earlier	41.	42.
43.	44.	45.	46.	47. best
48.	49.	50. less	51.	52.

Exercise 4: Write the correct form of the adjective or adverb in parentheses in the blank to complete each sentence.

53. James drew the _____ lines of all the students. (straight)

54. Our swim team did _____ than the opposing team. (well)

55. Joe was a _____ reader than my sister. (good)

56. Jeanne is the _____ of the two hairdressers. (careful)

57. He was the _____ decorated war hero of all. (frequently)

Exercise 5: Answer these definition questions.

58. Name the three main conjunctions. _____
59. Words that are joined with a conjunction are called _____.
60. Name two interjections. _____

CHAPTER 7 LESSON 3 APPLICATION TEST
(Student Page 63)

Exercise 1: Classify each sentence.

1. _____ Ducks and whales do not breathe under water.

2. _____ The sick children at the hospital clapped and shouted with delight at the funny clowns.

3. _____ A young boy and his sisters stopped and shopped at the new grocery store.

Directions: Complete the noun job table. Use Sentence 2.

List the Noun Used	List the Noun Job	Singular or Plural	Common or Proper
4.	5.	6.	7.
8.	9.	10.	11.
12.	13.	14.	15.
16.	17.	18.	19.

Exercise 2: Underline the negative words and write two ways to correct each double negative.

20. My aunt hasn't spent none of her extra money.
    21.
    22.

23. I don't want nothing from the store.
    24.
    25.

Exercise 3: Write the correct form of the adjective or adverb in parentheses in the blank to complete each sentence.

26. Today my taco salad was _____ than it was yesterday. (big)
27. These math problems are the _____ I've ever done. (easy)
28. He had the _____ of all the doctors. (responsibility)
29. The two girls worked _____ together. (well)
30. Janice worked _____ than Jill did. (well)

Exercise 4:   Editing Paragraph
Find each error and write the correction. Replace words underlined once with a synonym. Use the Editing Guide to help you. **Editing Guide: Homonyms:** 3 **Synonyms:** 3 **A/An:** 3 **Misspelled Words:** 3 **Capitals:** 26 **Subject-Verb Agreement:** 1 **Commas:** 2 **Apostrophes:** 1 **Periods:** 9 **Double Negatives:** 1 **End Marks:** 4

   i was <u>surprised</u> when mom <u>bought</u> a ibm computer from b j evans because my mom dont

no nothing about computors mr evans sent a expert mr p c sims to help my mom get started

mr sims spent to hours with mom and her computer the next day mr sims and mr evans

brough mom a new typewriter with an <u>big</u> red ribon and picked up there ibm computer

Level 7 Skill and Application Test Workbook

CHAPTER 8 LESSON 1 SKILL TEST A
(Student Page 66)

Exercise 1: Match the definitions. Write the correct letter beside each concept in the first column.

_____	1. all the predicate parts	A.	inverted order
_____	2. all the subject parts	B.	homonyms
_____	3. adjective questions	C.	person, place, or thing
_____	4. adverb questions	D.	subject noun or subject pronoun
_____	5. declarative sentence	E.	verb, adjective, or another adverb
_____	6. predicate words in the subject	F.	noun markers
_____	7. simple predicate	G.	a, an, the
_____	8. simple subject	H.	who
_____	9. words pronounced the same but different in meaning	I.	subject, verb, end mark, capital letter, complete sense
_____	10. words opposite in meaning	J.	statement
_____	11. words with the same meaning	K.	period
_____	12. the 5 parts of a sentence	L.	noun or a pronoun
_____	13. noun	M.	what kind, which one, how many
_____	14. subject noun question (person)	N.	period, statement, declarative sentence
_____	15. subject noun question (animal, place, thing)	O.	strong feeling
_____	16. verb	P.	complete predicate
_____	17. verb question	Q.	antonyms
_____	18. what the adverb modifies	R.	complete subject
_____	19. what the adjective modifies	S.	what
_____	20. 3 article adjectives	T.	exclamation point
_____	21. article adjectives can be called	U.	verb
_____	22. punctuation for declarative sentence	V.	tells what the subject does
_____	23. Q & A Flow for declarative sentence	W.	how, when, where
_____	24. exclamatory sentence shows	X.	what is being said about the subject
_____	25. punctuation for exclamatory sentence	Y.	synonyms

Exercise 2: Write 30 prepositions in the blanks below.

1.	11.	21.
2.	12.	22.
3.	13.	23.
4.	14.	24.
5.	15.	25.
6.	16.	26.
7.	17.	27.
8.	18.	28.
9.	19.	29.
10.	20.	30.

Level 7 Skill and Application Test Workbook

CHAPTER 8 LESSON 2 SKILL TEST B
(Student Page 70)

Exercise 1: In the parentheses at the end of each sentence, underline the part you will have to add to make a complete sentence. On a sheet of notebook paper, write complete sentences by adding the parts needed.

1. under the porch in the backyard   (subject part, predicate part, both the subject and predicate)
2. screeched and squealed on the concrete   (subject part, predicate part, both the subject and predicate)
3. before the final buzzer sounded   (subject part, predicate part, both the subject and predicate)
4. soared high above the trees   (subject part, predicate part, both the subject and predicate)
5. the soft white feather from the baby owl (subject part, predicate part, both the subject and predicate)

Exercise 2: Put a slash to separate each run-on sentence. Then, on your notebook paper, correct the run-on sentences as indicated by the labels in parentheses at the end of each sentence.

6. Lindsay is going to space camp in May her class is going, too. (SCS)
7. Katie enjoyed the movie she didn't like the restaurant. (CD, but)
8. Payton was frightened by the zoo animals he wanted to see them again. (CD, yet)
9. Dean grows vegetables in his garden he shares them with his friends. (CD;)
10. I didn't need any more books I bought one anyway. (CD; however)
11. Ashley's grandma hid eggs in the front yard Ashley's grandpa hid eggs in the front yard, too. (SCS)
12. The blue paint spilled on the floor the blue paint splashed on the carpet. (SCV)

Exercise 3: Identify each kind of sentence by writing the abbreviation in the blank. **(S, F, SCS, SCV, CD)**

_____ 13. My grandmother does cross-stitch and makes quilts as a hobby.
_____ 14. Karen owns a stable, and she gives riding lessons on weekends.
_____ 15. New Orleans and Miami are important coastal cities in America.
_____ 16. Coffee bushes grow well in shade. Corn does not grow well in shade.
_____ 17. We rented two movies, but we only watched one of them.
_____ 18. The Indians of the forests of North America.
_____ 19. Ice cream is a solid; buttermilk is a liquid.
_____ 20. Dan found fishing worms under rocks and logs.

Exercise 4: Use the 2 complete thoughts in bold print to write the kind of sentence listed below.

the pioneer men built log cabins / the pioneer women made clothing

21. (S,S) _____

22. (CD, and) _____

23. (CD;) _____

24. (SCS and CV) _____

25. (CD; however,) _____

Exercise 5: Write three compound sentences using these labels to guide you: (CD, conj) (CD; connective adverb) (CD;)

Level 7 Skill and Application Test Workbook

CHAPTER 8 LESSON 3 APPLICATION TEST A
(Student Page 71)

Exercise 1: Classify each sentence

1. _____ During the summer clumps of weeds grow in abundance along the river's edge.

2. _____ Jason and Justin grinned broadly and waited patiently for the final scene of the play.

3. _____ That amazing football player was not sent to the sidelines for the entire season.

Directions: Complete the noun job table. Use Sentence 2.

List the Noun Used	List the Noun Job	Singular or Plural	Common or Proper
4.	5.	6.	7.
8.	9.	10.	11.
12.	13.	14.	15.
16.	17.	18.	19.

Exercise 2: Identify each kind of sentence by writing the abbreviation in the blank. **(S, F, SCS, SCV, CD)**

_____ 20. We ate biscuits and drank juice for our breakfast.

_____ 21. In the car on the way to Florida for summer vacation.

_____ 22. My dad jogged down the street and up the hill.

_____ 23. The flashlight needed batteries, so Dad bought some at the store.

_____ 24. Monarch butterflies and honeybees search for nectar.

_____ 25. Apples are growing on the trees. Pumpkins are growing on the vine.

_____ 26. We persisted in our search; our efforts were rewarded.

Exercise 3: Use the 2 complete thoughts in bold print to write each kind of sentence listed below.

Ron painted the boat / he replaced the sails

27. (SCV) _____

28. (CD, and) _____

29. (CD;) _____

30. (CD; likewise,) _____

Exercise 4:   **Editing Paragraph**
Find each error and write the correction. Replace words underlined once with a synonym and words underlined twice with an antonym. Use the Editing Guide to help you. **Editing Guide: Synonyms: 1   Antonyms: 1   A/An: 1   Misspelled Words: 1   Capitals: 20   Subject-Verb Agreement: 4   Commas: 1   Underline: 1   Periods: 3   End Marks: 3**

the new jersey football team ride down main street and turn south on capital avenue mayor davis greets them with a <u>frown</u> and introduce them to an <u>young</u> reporter from the daily news then the mayor introduce the athletic directer and mr b j wise the football coach of the university of new jersey wildcats

© SHURLEY INSTRUCTIONAL MATERIALS, INC.

CHAPTER 8 LESSON 3 APPLICATION TEST B
(Student Page 72)

Exercise 1: Match the definitions. Write the correct letter beside each concept in the first column.

_____	1. Q & A Flow for exclamatory sentence	A.	question mark
_____	2. word that starts the complete predicate	B.	helping verbs
_____	3. adverb that comes right before the verb	C.	one- or two-word exclamation
_____	4. preposition	D.	apostrophe
_____	5. name of noun/pronoun after a preposition	E.	subject noun, object of the preposition
_____	6. the 7 subject pronouns	F.	question sentence
_____	7. understood subject pronoun	G.	nouns showing ownership
_____	8. imperative sentence	H.	verb
_____	9. punctuation for imperative sentence	I.	my, our, his, her, its, their, your
_____	10. Q & A Flow for imperative sentence	J.	adverb
_____	11. the 7 object pronouns	K.	adjective
_____	12. 2 noun jobs	L.	two or more words joined by a conjunction
_____	13. the 7 possessive pronouns	M.	object of the preposition
_____	14. possessive noun	N.	period, command, imperative sentence
_____	15. punctuation mark for possessive noun	O.	I, we, he, she, it, they, you,
_____	16. the possessive question	P.	and, but, or
_____	17. verbs in front of a main verb	Q.	command
_____	18. part of speech for *NOT*	R.	period
_____	19. interrogative sentence	S.	you
_____	20. punctuation for interrogative sentence	T.	adverb exception
_____	21. Q & A Flow for interrogative sentence	U.	me, us, him, her, it, them, you
_____	22. 3 main conjunctions	V.	whose
_____	23. compound	W.	exclamation point, strong feeling, exclamatory sentence
_____	24. interjection	X.	connects a noun or a pronoun to the rest of the sentence
_____	25. part of speech for a possessive noun	Y.	question mark, question, interrogative sentence

Exercise 2: Write the 8 forms of the verb *be* in the blanks below.

26.	28.	30.	32.
27.	29.	31.	33.

Exercise 3: Write the 15 other helping verbs in the blanks below.

34.	39.	44.
35.	40.	45.
36.	41.	46.
37.	42.	47.
38.	43.	48.

CHAPTER 9 LESSON 1 SKILL TEST A
(Student Page 75)

Exercise 1: Write the correct answer to each definition question in the blanks below.

1. What does a noun name? _____
2. What question do you ask to find the subject noun if the sentence is about a person? _____
3. What question do you ask to find the subject if the sentence is not about a person? _____
4. What word tells what the subject does or what the subject is? _____
5. What question do you ask in the Q & A Flow to find the verb? _____
6. What does an adverb modify? _____
7. What are the adverb questions? _____
8. What does an adjective modify? _____
9. What are the adjective questions? _____
10. What are the three article adjectives? _____
11. What is a declarative sentence? _____
12. What is an exclamatory sentence? _____
13. What word usually starts the complete predicate? _____
14. What are all the parts in the subject of a sentence called? _____
15. What are all the parts in the predicate of a sentence called? _____
16. What is an adverb exception? _____
17. What is a preposition? _____
18. What is an object of the preposition? _____
19. Name the 7 subject pronouns. _____

Writing Assignment
Use the descriptive writing steps and the descriptive outline in Chapter 7 to do the writing assignment below. After you have finished writing your paragraph, put it in your Rough Draft folder.

Writing Assignment #12: Descriptive Paragraph in First Person
Topic: Freedom
Logical narrowed topic: What Freedom Means to Me
Writing Topic: What Freedom Means to Me
Or Choose: What Freedom Means to My Family

CHAPTER 9 LESSON 2 SKILL TEST B
(Student Page 77)

Exercise 1: In the parentheses at the end of each sentence, underline the part you will have to add to make a complete sentence. On a sheet of notebook paper, write complete sentences by adding the parts needed.

1. because Charles locked the door   (subject part, predicate part, both the subject and predicate)
2. while Susan took a nap   (subject part, predicate part, both the subject and predicate)
3. at the computer desk in her office   (subject part, predicate part, both the subject and predicate)
4. unless our group works hard on this project (subject part, predicate part, both the subject and predicate)
5. watered the seeds and watched them grow (subject part, predicate part, both the subject and predicate)

Exercise 2: Put a slash to separate each run-on sentence. Then, on your notebook paper, correct the run-on sentences as indicated by the labels in parentheses at the end of each sentence.

6. The couple sat in the front they could see their son. (CX, where, 2)
7. My car is small we can all crowd into it. (CX, although, 1)
8. The math student was confused he did not ask questions. (CD; however, 2)
9. The small child did not understand he could not have more candy. (CX, why, 2)
10. The dance troupe danced to classical music they sang beautiful songs. (SCV)
11. You are kind to others they will think highly of you. (CX, if, 1)
12. The young man sold his furniture he moved to a new state. (SCV)

Exercise 3: Identify each kind of sentence by writing the abbreviation in the blank. **(S, F, SCS, SCV, CD, CX)**

_____ 13. After we swam for several hours, we were ready for a big meal.
_____ 14. The vet gave Bingo a shot and some antibiotic pills.
_____ 15. Pamela took notes on her topic, and she wrote her essay last night.
_____ 16. Where my group sits in the library, I must sit.
_____ 17. Though you are captain of the team.
_____ 18. The dictionary gives definitions and offers pronunciations of words.
_____ 19. Brown bats were living in the cave that we explored.
_____ 20. Even though I try to avoid illness, the flu bug always finds me.

Exercise 4: Use the 2 complete thoughts in bold print to write each kind of sentence listed below.

the buzzer sounds / the game is over

21. (CX, if, 1)

22. (CX, when, 2)

23. (CD, and)

24. (CX, as soon as, 1)

25. (S,S)

Exercise 5: Write two complex sentences.

CHAPTER 9 LESSON 3 APPLICATION TEST A
(Student Page 78)

Exercise 1: Classify each sentence.

1. _____ Yesterday the hungry wolves were howling outside the horses' corral by our house.

2. _____ Do comets travel around the sun in egg-shaped paths?

3. _____ My brother and his friends are flying to Louisiana tomorrow for the soccer tournament.

Directions: Complete the noun job table. Use Sentence 1.

List the Noun Used	List the Noun Job	Singular or Plural	Common or Proper
4.	5.	6.	7.
8.	9.	10.	11.
12.	13.	14.	15.
16.	17.	18.	19.

Exercise 2: Identify each kind of sentence by writing the abbreviation in the blank. **(S, F, SCS, SCV, CD, CX)**

_____ 20. The mischievous toddler giggled whenever he saw his mother.
_____ 21. Because the morning fog was thick, we drove to Grandpa's in the afternoon.
_____ 22. Mom bought a quilt and some jelly at the fair.
_____ 23. The men worked hard for their boss; therefore, they received an extra bonus.
_____ 24. Unless we buy our fireworks today.
_____ 25. We think of the South when we think of cotton.
_____ 26. Since you spent an hour in the library.

Exercise 3: Use the 2 complete thoughts in bold print to write each kind of sentence listed below.

Tom is a skilled mechanic / he has opened his own repair shop

27. (CX, because, 1) _____

28. (CD, and) _____

29. (SCV) _____

Exercise 4:   Editing Paragraph
Find each error and write the correction. Use the Editing Guide to help you. **Editing Guide: Homonyms: 1   A/An: 1
Misspelled Words: 4   Capitals: 19   Subject-Verb Agreement: 4   Commas: 7   Periods: 4   End Marks: 3**

   dr j d park an former investigater for the department of justice now teach sience world history I and spanish at liberty high school in brooklyn new york since dr park have degrees in several study areas he is qualifed too do many diferent jobs however he like teaching best because he love helping kids learn

CHAPTER 9 LESSON 3 APPLICATION TEST B
(Student Page 79)

Exercise 1: Write the correct answer to each definition question in the blanks below.

1. Name two noun jobs. _____
2. Name the understood subject pronoun. _____
3. What is an imperative sentence? _____
4. What is the punctuation mark used at the end of an imperative sentence? _____
5. Name the 7 object pronouns. _____
6. Name the 7 possessive pronouns. _____
7. What does a possessive noun show? _____
8. What one punctuation mark does a possessive noun always have? _____
9. What 2 jobs does a possessive noun have? _____
10. What question do you ask to find possessive words? _____
11. Where are helping verbs found? _____
12. Name the 8 forms of the *be* verb. _____
13. What part of speech is the word NOT? _____
14. What is an interrogative sentence? _____
15. What is the punctuation mark used at the end of an interrogative sentence? _____
16. Name the three main conjunctions. _____
17. What are 2 subjects or 2 verbs called? _____
18. What is a 1-or 2-word exclamation called? _____
19. What is a natural sentence order? _____
20. What is an inverted order? _____
21. Show 3 ways to join a CD sentence. _____
22. Name the 2 sentences found in a CX sentence. _____
23. What are the names of the two kinds of sentences that are joined by coordinate conjunctions and subordinate conjunctions? _____

CHAPTER 10 LESSON 2 SKILL TEST A
(Student Page 85)

Exercise 1: In the parentheses at the end of each sentence, underline the part you will have to add to make a complete sentence. On a sheet of notebook paper, write complete sentences by adding the parts needed.

1. howled and bayed at the moon (subject part, predicate part, both the subject and predicate)
2. the sparkling chandelier with hundreds of crystals (subject part, predicate part, both the subject and predicate)
3. under the hammock next to the maple tree (subject part, predicate part, both the subject and predicate)
4. children of all races and nationalities (subject part, predicate part, both the subject and predicate)

Exercise 2: Put a slash to separate each run-on sentence. Then, on the lines provided, correct the run-on sentences as indicated by the labels in parentheses at the end of each sentence.

5. Paratroopers landed on the grass the audience clapped. (CX, when, 1)

6. Jeanne drives carefully down the mountain Joseph drives down the mountain. (SCS)

7. Laura likes to cook supper she dislikes washing the dishes. (CD, but)

8. Dale crawled under the ledge Dale crawled across the fallen tree. (SCPrep)

9. We sold 500 pounds of shrimp we did not make enough money. (CX, although, 1)

10. Huge mosquitoes buzzed in our ears they bit our bare legs. (SCV)

Exercise 3: Identify the kind of sentence by writing the abbreviations in the blank. **(S, F, SCS, SCV, CD, CX)**

_____ 11. Scott paints landscapes in art class, but Martin sculpts with clay.
_____ 12. Kirk races motorcycles and flies model airplanes.
_____ 13. Randy studied for his exam until Vanessa called him for dinner.
_____ 14. Jennifer is having fun at band camp; however, she misses her friends.
_____ 15. The charming yellow cottage by the sea in the summertime.

Exercise 4: Use the 2 complete thoughts in bold print to write each kind of sentence listed below.

the female rabbit lines her burrow with fur / she keeps her babies warm

16. (CD, and)

17. (SCV)

18. (CD;)

19. (CX, because, 1)

CHAPTER 10 LESSON 2 SKILL TEST B
(Student Page 86)

Exercise 1: Rewrite this paragraph. Correct fragments and improve the short, choppy sentences by using a combination of simple, compound, and complex sentences. Underline simple sentences once, compound sentences twice, and put parentheses around the complex sentences. **Sentence Guide for every two sentences:** (SCV) (CX, because, 1) (SCS-CD, but) (CX, because, 2)

Amanda fell out of bed. Amanda broke her arm. Amanda has a cast on her right arm. Amanda doesn't have to do her homework. Amanda's brother is jealous. Amanda's sister is jealous. Amanda's brother and sister would not want to break their arms to get out of homework. Amanda cannot wait to get her cast off. Never minded homework, anyway.

Exercise 2: Rewrite this paragraph. Correct fragments and improve the short, choppy sentences by using a combination of simple, compound, and complex sentences. Underline simple sentences once, compound sentences twice, and put parentheses around the complex sentences. **Sentence Guide for every two sentences:** (SCS) *(SCOP) (CD, but) (CX, since, 1) (CX, when, 2) (*SCOP means simple sentence with a compound object of the preposition.)

The tired donkeys plodded along the dusty trail. The hot, sweaty horses plodded along, too. In the heat the exhausted travelers looked for shade trees. The travelers looked for a cool stream. Their eyes searched the desert horizon desperately for shelter from the scorching heat. There was no relief in sight. Nature's lessons were harsh. Second chances were rare. However, the travelers got lucky. Found water and survived.

Exercise 3: On notebook paper, write a paragraph using *dancing* as your topic. Use a combination of simple, compound, and complex sentences throughout the paragraph. Underline simple sentences once, compound sentences twice, and put parentheses around the complex sentences.

CHAPTER 10 LESSON 3 APPLICATION TEST
(Student Page 87)

Exercise 1: Classify each sentence.

1. _____ Tommy could not finish the crossword puzzle by himself.

2. _____ A large wolf can break a sheep's neck with one savage snap!

3. _____ For breakfast I like ham and eggs with a piece of toast.

Directions: Complete the noun job table. Use Sentence 2.

List the Noun Used	List the Noun Job	Singular or Plural	Common or Proper
4.	5.	6.	7.
8.	9.	10.	11.
12.	13.	14.	15.
16.	17.	18.	19.

Exercise 2: Identify the kind of sentence by writing the abbreviations in the blank. **(S, F, SCS, SCV, CD, CX)**

_____ 20. At the beginning of my history class.

_____ 21. Our science class gathered plants from the forest; we made terrariums at school.

_____ 22. Jay writes instructions and designs pictures for manuals.

_____ 23. Joyce planted seeds in her vegetable garden and in her flower garden.

_____ 24. Although the worried lady searched frantically for her jewelry, she did not find it.

_____ 25. I baked chocolate brownies while Dad washed the car.

Exercise 3: On your notebook paper, rewrite this paragraph. Correct fragments and improve the short, choppy sentences by using a combination of simple, compound, and complex sentences. Underline simple sentences once, compound sentences twice, and put parentheses around the complex sentences.

   Scotty ate two donuts for his breakfast. Levi ate six donuts for his breakfast. Scotty enjoyed his donuts. Levi got a stomach ache. Levi moaned all morning at school. Levi groaned all morning, too. Finally, Levi's teacher had Scotty take Levi to the nurse's office. Scotty told the nurse about the donuts. She understood why Levi had a stomach ache. Promised the nurse that he would never eat so many donuts again. Levi promised Scotty the same thing. Left the office. Unhappy but wiser,

Exercise 4:   Editing Paragraph
Find each error and write the correction. Replace words underlined once with a synonym. Use the Editing Guide to help you. **Editing Guide: Homonyms: 5   Synonyms: 3   A/An: 1   Misspelled Words: 3   Capitals: 22   Subject-Verb Agreement: 2   Commas: 5   Apostrophes: 2   Periods: 3   End Marks: 6**

   mr p t armstrong my uncle on my mothers side of the family was a expert on king arthur

i had herd storys all my life about king arthur my sisters and i had memorised how each

story started and we actualy learned a lot of history by listening to my uncles <u>stories</u> king

arthur was the <u>strong</u> and noble leader of the knights at camelot england these english

knights road too the rescue of those in need king arthur and his nights was called the knights

of the round table and they was known for there <u>courage</u> and goodness

CHAPTER 11 LESSON 1 SKILL TEST A
(Student Page 91)

Exercise 1: In the blank beside each statement below, write **F** if the statement is a fact or **O** if the statement is an opinion.

_____ 1. Fire needs air in order to burn.

_____ 2. The food in the cafeteria is terrible.

_____ 3. Sally will make a good class president.

_____ 4. Casey scored two touchdowns in the game Friday night.

_____ 5. I go to Washington Junior High School.

_____ 6. George Washington was the first president of the United States.

_____ 7. Kittens are cuter than puppies.

_____ 8. Everyone loves puppies because they're adorable.

_____ 9. We bought new shop equipment yesterday.

_____ 10. This is an excellent school.

_____ 11. The Liberty Bell is in Philadelphia, Pennsylvania.

_____ 12. Nature's Best cereal is the healthiest new cereal on the market today.

_____ 13. Most people hate spinach.

_____ 14. This steak house serves the best food in the state.

_____ 15. Everyone loves to travel.

Exercise 2: In the blanks below, write the number(s) of the propaganda technique(s) used in each message.
(1 - Loaded Words, 2 - Famous People, 3 - Everybody Does It, 4 - Mudslinging, 5 - Fact/Opinion)

_____ 1. Are you tired of batteries that don't last? Buy Long Life Batteries the next time you buy.

_____ 2. Arkansas leads the nation in growing rice. Arkansas rice tastes the best!

_____ 3. A vote for Alice Duncan is a vote for education!

_____ 4. Hundreds of farmers in Michigan rely on *Agriculture Today* to keep them informed about current agricultural issues. Do the smart thing. Subscribe to this informative magazine today!

_____ 5. Six thousand people attended the fund raiser. It was a huge success!

_____ 6. Public education, health care, taxes, the environment. Governor Johnson cares about the things that are important to you.

_____ 7. Actress Diana Doll uses Silky Smooth Shampoo to keep her hair shiny and beautiful. Don't you want beautiful, healthy hair like Diana Doll?

CHAPTER 11 LESSON 2 SKILL TEST B
(Student Page 93)

Exercise 1: In the parentheses at the end of each sentence, underline the part you will have to add to make a complete sentence. On a sheet of notebook paper, write complete sentences by adding the parts needed.

1. the apples and oranges in those crates   (subject part, predicate part, both the subject and predicate)
2. swung and missed the buzzing flies   (subject part, predicate part, both the subject and predicate)
3. baked delicious pies and cakes   (subject part, predicate part, both the subject and predicate)
4. if we clean our mess in the kitchen   (subject part, predicate part, both the subject and predicate)
5. fought and won their battle on the soccer field   (subject part, predicate part, both the subject and predicate)

Exercise 2: Put a slash to separate each run-on sentence. Then, on the lines provided, correct the run-on sentences as indicated by the labels in parentheses at the end of each sentence. (**CParts** means compound parts in the sentence.)

6. The young artist received special paints for his birthday he got a set of brushes, too. (SCParts)
_____

7. The snake slithered across the grass it slithered under the woodpile. (SCParts)
_____

8. The young artist received special paints for his birthday he got a set of brushes, too. (CD, and)
_____

9. The snake slithered across the grass it slithered under the woodpile. (CX, after, 1)
_____

10. I cannot run in the race I have warmed up. (CX, until, 2)
_____

Exercise 3: Identify the kind of sentence by writing the abbreviations in the blank. **(S, F, SCS, SCV, CD, CX)**

_____ 11. Mother's coffee had sugar and cream in it.
_____ 12. I could hear the bass on his radio as he drove down the street.
_____ 13. Mother likes her coffee with sugar and cream in it.
_____ 14. Because I was the most qualified, I was offered the management position in our office.
_____ 15. The big ship beyond the pier and across the waterway.
_____ 16. The farmer planted soybeans, and his neighbor planted milo.

Exercise 4: Use the 2 complete thoughts in bold print to write each kind of sentence listed below.

I read and studied for three hours / I made an A on my test

17. (CX, because, 1) _____

18. (CD; therefore) _____

19. (SCV) _____

20. (CX, before, 2) _____

Exercise 5: Write a simple sentence, a compound sentence, and a complex sentence and identify them with these labels: **(S) (CD) (CX)**. The simple sentence can have compound parts, but you must identify the compound parts in the label: **(SCV) (SCS) (SCParts)**.

CHAPTER 11 LESSON 2 SKILL TEST C
(Student Page 94)

Directions for Exercises 1-2: Identify each thought below by putting a slash between each one. Then, rewrite the paragraph. Use the *Guidelines for Combining Sentences* in Chapter 10 to combine related thoughts to make compound, complex, or simple sentences with compound parts. Avoid overusing the conjunctions *and, but*, and *so*. Underline simple sentences once, compound sentences twice, and put parentheses around the complex sentences.

Exercise 1:

My mother is teaching my brother how to cook and my brother's friends are giving him a lot of sympathy because they feel sorry for him slaving away in the kitchen however, my mother is a smart woman she starts my brother's cooking education with fudge, cookies, and cakes and now my brother's friends are asking if they can come over to join him in the kitchen and they have suddenly seen the value of learning to cook and yes, my mother is certainly a wise woman.

_____

_____

_____

_____

_____

_____

_____

Exercise 2:

I went with my big sister, the cowgirl, to the horse show last week to help out and I can't understand why she loves horse shows and rodeos because they are hot and noisy and smelly and I got tired of washing horses brushing horses and riding horses but my sister seemed to enjoy all the dust and confusion and in fact, she talked and laughed with all the cowboys and actually had a great time and I just don't understand girls, especially my sister!

_____

_____

_____

_____

_____

_____

_____

Exercise 3: On a sheet of notebook paper, write a paragraph using *Three Ways to Have a Great Day* as your topic. Underline simple sentences once, compound sentences twice, and put parentheses around the complex sentences.

CHAPTER 11 LESSON 3 APPLICATION TEST
(Student Page 95)

Exercise 1: Classify each sentence.

1. _____ Instantly the aroma of the popcorn filled the room!

2. _____ Dad parked his new car in the parking lot rather carefully before the big meeting.

3. _____ Did your brother borrow our lawnmower yesterday?

Directions: Complete the noun job table. Use Sentence 2.

List the Noun Used	List the Noun Job	Singular or Plural	Common or Proper
4.	5.	6.	7.
8.	9.	10.	11.
12.	13.	14.	15.
16.	17.	18.	19.

Exercise 2: Identify each kind of sentence by writing the abbreviations in the blank. **(S, F, SCS, SCV, CD, CX)**

_____ 20. The grouchy man grumbled when he saw the neighborhood dogs in his yard.

_____ 21. Steam rose invitingly from the hot cup of hot chocolate.

_____ 22. An oxygen tank sat dangerously close to the flame, but no one noticed.

_____ 23. The windows rattled and shook from the blast of dynamite.

_____ 24. Until the fire department arrived, the grass fire was out of control.

Exercise 3:   Editing Paragraph
Find each error and write the correction. Replace words underlined once with a synonym. Use the Editing Guide to help you. **Editing Guide: Synonyms: 2 Misspelled Words: 4 Capitals: 28 Periods: 5 Commas: 8 Apostrophes: 1 Quotations: 2 End Marks: 4**

we expect mom and dad to arrive in dallas texas on the fourth of july with dr o g frog the presedent of the univrsity in lily pond england mr frog is staying with us while he is in dallas for the <u>annual</u> amphibians anonymous convention dr frog a man of <u>many</u> talents will provide entertanment at the conventin he will sing the crazy hit song im croaking over you leap frog

Exercise 4: Identify each thought below by putting a slash between each one. Then, rewrite the paragraph on a sheet of notebook paper. Correct fragments and improve the long, rambling sentences by using different kinds of sentences. Underline simple sentences once, compound sentences twice, and put parentheses around the complex sentences.

My alarm clock hates me because it will not go off when it should go off and it goes off when it should not go off in the middle of the night my faithful mechanical tormentor rings loud clear and long and then early the next morning there is total silence and I am always late for school and I am blurry-eyed from hearing that alarm all during the night but I have finally found the perfect place for my pesky little alarm clock because I have given it to my pesky little brother because they deserve each other.

CHAPTER 12 LESSON 2 SKILL TEST
(Student Page 103)

Exercise 1: In the parentheses at the end of each sentence, underline the part you need to add to make a complete sentence. On a sheet of notebook paper, write complete sentences by adding the parts needed.

1. while we sang songs around the campfire   (subject part, predicate part, both the subject and predicate)
2. during the blizzard at the top of the mountain   (subject part, predicate part, both the subject and predicate)
3. a nutritious snack of peanut butter and crackers (subject part, predicate part, both the subject and predicate)

Exercise 2: Put a slash to separate each run-on sentence. Then, on the lines provided, correct the run-on sentences as indicated by the labels in parentheses at the end of each sentence.

4. Buster patiently herds the sheep into the pen he is a good sheepdog. (CX, because, 2)
_____

5. Worker ants feed the queen ant they take care of her eggs. (CD, and)
_____

6. The beginning skiers learned from their instructor they did not ski down the small slope. (CX, until, 1)
_____

Exercise 3: Identify each kind of sentence by writing the abbreviations in the blank. **(S, F, SCS, SCV, CD, CX)**

_____   7. The noisy jalopy sputtered and jerked down the street.

_____   8. The teacher permitted her class to watch the election returns while they ate their lunch.

_____   9. We hurried down the aisle; consequently, we found some good seats.

Exercise 4: Use the 2 complete thoughts in bold print to write each kind of sentence listed below.

Mom and Dad jog every morning / they are losing weight

10. (CX, since, 1) _____

11. (CD, so) _____

12. (CD; thus) _____

Exercise 5: Identify each thought below by putting a slash between each one. Then, rewrite the paragraph. Use the *Guidelines for Combining Sentences* in Chapter 10 to combine related thoughts to make compound, complex, or simple sentences with compound parts. Avoid overusing the conjunctions *and, but,* and *so.* Underline simple sentences once, compound sentences twice, and put parentheses around the complex sentences.

    The weather is cold today and the weather is damp today and I had big plans today but the weather is not cooperating and this morning I called the weather station to get a weather report and the weatherman predicts rain this afternoon and the weatherman predicts sleet this afternoon and I am so disappointed because I will have to cancel my hiking expedition with my friends and I will probably end up sitting in front of the TV moaning and groaning and that is why I do not want it to rain or sleet today.

Exercise 6: Write a simple sentence, a compound sentence, and a complex sentence and identify them with these labels: **(S) (CD) (CX).** The simple sentence can have compound parts, but you must identify the compound parts in the label: **(SCV) (SCS) (SCParts).**

CHAPTER 12 LESSON 3 APPLICATION TEST
(Student Page 104)

Exercise 1: Mixed Patterns 1-2. Classify each sentence.

1. _____ Some mining practices have caused serious environmental problems to our landscape.

2. _____ Write your name in the upper corner of your paper.

3. _____ The young pianist flew to the concert from a small town in Italy.

Directions: Complete the noun job table. Use Sentence 3.

List the Noun Used	List the Noun Job	Singular or Plural	Common or Proper
4.	5.	6.	7.
8.	9.	10.	11.
12.	13.	14.	15.
16.	17.	18.	19.

Exercise 2: Identify each kind of sentence by writing the abbreviations in the blank. **(S, F, SCS, SCV, CD, CX)**

_____ 20. Although the trip was long, the travelers were cheerful and excited.

_____ 21. Cody was sleepy, but he would not go to bed.

_____ 22. Ed and Mary owned a small restaurant on the outskirts of town.

_____ 23. The jeweler designed pendants and rings from gold and precious gems.

_____ 24. The audience could not hear because the sound system was turned off.

Exercise 3:   **Editing Paragraph**

Find each error and write the correction. Replace words underlined once with a synonym. Use the Editing Guide to help you. **Editing Guide: Homonyms: 1   Synonyms: 1   Misspelled Words: 3   Capitals: 23   Subject-Verb Agreement: 1   Periods: 1   Commas: 7   Apostrophes: 2   End Marks: 3**

    on monday june 13 i hope too visit johns brother tom c alexander because tom lives near the alantic ocean in miami florida while i am in florida i hope to visit disneyworld and sea world in orlando toms family know how to have <u>fun</u> and i am looking foreward to my vacatison with them

Exercise 4: Identify each thought below by putting a slash between each one. Then, rewrite the paragraph on notebook paper. Correct fragments and improve long, rambling sentences by using different kinds of sentences. Underline simple sentences once, compound sentences twice, and put parentheses around the complex sentences.

    I am a strong, good-looking young man in his junior high prime and I have suddenly realized how important it is to eat a good nourishing breakfast in the mornings so that I will be able to take an early morning jog around the block in my muscle shirt and jogging shorts and my mom loves my sudden interest in health and exercise but she has become suspicious since she realized my early morning jogging takes me right by the cheerleaders' early-morning practice session grins at me now when I fuss over which running outfit to wear.

CHAPTER 13 LESSON 2 SKILL TEST
(Student Page 113)

Exercise 1: Use the Quotation Rules to help punctuate the quotations below. Underline the explanatory words.

1. taylor shouted hey chad did you see that huge spider that crawled into tinas desk

2. hey chad did you see that huge spider that crawled into tinas desk taylor shouted

3. hey chad taylor shouted did you see that huge spider that crawled into tinas desk

4. hey chad taylor shouted did you see that huge spider that crawled into tinas desk lets warn her

5. the frightened girl said weakly im lost and hungry

6. our ship is beginning to take on water grumbled the captain

7. i have no further questions for this witness said the lawyer

8. my parents are chaperones billy groaned dad says he and mom are even going to dance

9. would you care for any dessert mrs smith the waitress asked politely

10. jake the teacher asked sternly wheres your homework

11. my new shoes hurt my feet whined the little girl to her mother

12. tomorrows lunch our teacher announced will be spaghetti salad and garlic bread

Exercise 2: **Editing Paragraph**
Find each error and write the correction. Use the Editing Guide to help you. **Editing Guide: Capitals: 41 Commas: 12 Periods: 6 Apostrophes: 7 Misspelled Words: 4 Quotations: 14 End Marks: 20**

    chad was desperete he was broke and his job hunting all morning had turned up nothing he needed money to pay for the football-training weekend next month as he checked off the rest of the rejections from his list of job posibilities mr wiser his next door neighbor drove up in his beat-up farm truck

    chad jumped up and ran across the street mr wiser i need an extra job do you have anything i can do to earn some money

    mr wiser grinned as he looked at the eager young man standing in front of him well chad i think i might be able to find a few extra things that need to be done on the farm since this is our busyest season ill pick you up in ten minutes tell your mom that you wont be back until about ten tonight

    wait chad exclaimed disappointedly to mr wiser i cant work that long the biggest game of the season is playing on tv tonight and id miss it

    life is full of tough choices mr wiser told him remember chad you have to work when the work is ready and not when youre ready see you in ten minutes or not at all

    as chad crawled wearily out of mr wisers truck at ten oclock he cluched the money he had earned he walked proudly through his front door and announced i have a full-time job for the rest of the summer

Level 7 Skill and Application Test Workbook

CHAPTER 13 LESSON 3 APPLICATION TEST
(Student Page 114)

Exercise 1: Classify each sentence.

1. _____ Tell me the company's address over the phone.

2. _____ Yesterday Sally's brother bought her a motorcycle for her birthday.

3. _____ Tom's friends at work gave him money for his operation.

Directions: Complete the noun job table. Use Sentence 3.

List the Noun Used	List the Noun Job	Singular or Plural	Common or Proper
4.	5.	6.	7.
8.	9.	10.	11.
12.	13.	14.	15.
16.	17.	18.	19.
20.	21.	22.	23.

Exercise 2: Use the Quotation Rules to help punctuate the quotations below. Underline the explanatory words.

24. the agent said jeff you must pay for your ticket in advance

25. jeff you must pay for your ticket in advance the agent said

26. jeff the agent said you must pay for your ticket in advance

27. you must pay for your ticket in advance jeff the agent said you may use your credit card

28. carol whispered i cant find my seat in this dark theater

29. yes we are ready chuckled mom to see your big surprise

30. now where wondered paul out loud have i put my baseball shoes

31. i paid good money for those shoes bellowed dad as andy tromped through the muddy yard then he added sympathetically as he saw andy slip and fall flat on his face on second thought why dont you go take a shower then you can come back and scrape the mud off your clothes and shoes by the way andy don't forget to wash your face

Exercise 3:   **Editing Paragraph**
Find each error and write the correction. Replace words underlined once with a synonym. Use the Editing Guide to help you. **Editing Guide:** Synonyms: 1   Misspelled Words: 4   Subject-Verb Agreement: 1   Capitals: 14   Periods: 1   Commas: 6   End Marks: 2   Underlining: 1

can we get joe t hill author of wild times to come to walton arena in fayetteville arkansas on july 5 1995 to <u>speak</u> to our english department i hope this distinguished speaker can come to our college campas because we will also invites the people in the fayetteville comunity and in the surounding areas

CHAPTER 14 LESSON 2 SKILL TEST
(Student Page 117)

Exercise 1: Use the Quotation Rules to help punctuate the quotations below. Underline the explanatory words.

1. whew sighed the old timer theres a storm blowing in from the north

2. there is a time limit for this test the teacher said calmly you have thirty minutes to complete it

3. oh no my favorite sweater is ruined wailed elaine

4. the travel guide said yes your flight will stop in atlanta and dallas before arriving in memphis

5. wow squealed the girls this water is too cold for swimming

6. maria giggled samson you are the silliest dog ive ever seen

7. sara smith the intercom crackled please report to the information desk immediately

Exercise 2: Edit the conversation below. **Editing Guide: Capitals: 11   End Marks: 6   Quotation Marks: 10   Commas: 8   Apostrophes: 4**

travis come look at my new car shouted sammy

why sammy replied travis this car doesnt look new at all its missing two doors and the top

oh travis sighed sammy dont you know this is a dune buggy hop in and ill take you for a spin

Exercise 3: Edit the conversation below. **Editing Guide: Capitals: 7   End Marks: 3   Commas: 5   Quotation Marks: 8   Apostrophes: 1**

skip the shop called to say your motorcycle is ready said lois to her brother

skip asked did they say how much the repair bill was

yes replied lois but i dont think you want to hear it

Exercise 4: Edit the conversation below. **Editing Guide: Capitals: 14   End Marks: 10   Commas: 7   Quotation Marks: 14   Apostrophes: 2**

hey joey kevin hollered across the fence to his best friend do you know what my big sister and her friends are having tonight they are having a no make-up no dress-up no boyfriend party

hmm i wonder what the girls would do if their boyfriends suddenly showed up asked joey

well laughed kevin maybe we should invite the boys and find out

this will be great fun exclaimed joey my sister wont even step outside the house without make-up so i cant wait to see what the girls do when their boyfriends show up and see them without make-up

Level 7 Skill and Application Test Workbook

CHAPTER 14 LESSON 3 APPLICATION TEST
(Student Page 118)

Exercise 1: Classify each sentence.

1. _____ My boss finally gave me a big raise and a big promotion!

2. _____ Cindy and Linda brought me a huge piece of birthday cake and a large cup of punch.

3. _____ Did you send Andy and Larry a singing telegram for their birthday present?

Directions: Complete the noun job table. Use Sentence 3.

List the Noun Used	List the Noun Job	Singular or Plural	Common or Proper
4.	5.	6.	7.
8.	9.	10.	11.
12.	13.	14.	15.
16.	17.	18.	19.

Exercise 2: Edit the story below. Use the Editing Guide to help you. **Editing Guide: Capitals: 20 Commas: 9 Quotations: 20 Apostrophes: 4 End Marks: 15**

mmm whats that wonderful smell exclaimed cindy

that smell happens to be my special homemade chocolate chip cookies replied the cook smugly

spencer my sweet brother wheedled cindy you make the best cookies i cant wait to eat some

wait a minute these cookies are going to cost you said spencer gleefully waving the plate of chocolate chip cookies under her nose

oh you make me so mad glared cindy all right whatever you think theyre worth

spencer said triumphantly you can have all these cookies if you and mark will take me along when you go to the movies tonight

well said cindy as she grinned and reached for a cookie thats a small price to pay are you buying the popcorn

Exercise 3:   Editing Paragraph
Find each error and write the correction. Use the Editing Guide to help you. **Editing Guide: Homonyms: 1 Capitals: 17 Apostrophes: 1 A/An: 1 Misspelled Words: 1 Subject-Verb Agreement: 1 Commas: 6 Underlining: 2 End Marks: 4**

my sister vonda and her family live in an small suburb north of cheyenne called big lake they have titled their small two-acre estate the ponderosa because they all love water sports vondas family keep a little boat at big daddy lake since my sister named there boat the titanic i have come to the concluion that they have all gone a little overboard on big names for small things

CHAPTER 15 LESSON 1 SKILL TEST A
(Student Page 124)

Exercise 1: In the numbered boxes below, write the five parts of a friendly letter.

Friendly Letter Parts

1.	2.	4.
Box or street City, state, zip code Date	Dear ____,	Your friend,
	3.	5.
		Writer's First and/or Last Name

Exercise 2: Draw a line to separate all the parts and sentences of the friendly letter in the box below. Then, on notebook paper, use the information from the Friendly Letter Information Box below to write a friendly letter in the correct form. Capitalize and punctuate as needed.

Friendly Letter Information Box

From: maria hernandez 341 southbend road great plains montana 89762 september 30 20____ dear carlos i am looking forward to my first winter in montana i am already wearing a sweater mexico seems so far away but I love it here ill write more later your sister

To: carlos garcia 1527 pablo drive mexico city mexico 99872

Exercise 3: In the numbered boxes below, write the two parts of an envelope used for a friendly letter.

Friendly Envelope Parts

1.	2.
Writer's Name Box or street City, state, zip code	Name of Receiver Box or street City, state, zip code

Exercise 4: On notebook paper, draw an envelope and use the parts in your Friendly Letter Information Box above to help you address the envelope correctly. Also, draw a stamp on your envelope.

Exercise 5: Answer these questions about the friendly letter and envelope you have just completed.

1. Who wrote the letter?
2. Who will receive the letter?
3. When was the letter written?
4. Where does the writer live?
5. What closing did the writer use?
6. What greeting did this writer use?
7. What is another word for greeting?
8. What name is in the mailing address?
9. What name is in the return address?
10. Where does the person receiving the letter live?
11. What is this letter about?
12. Did you draw a stamp on the envelope?
13. What are the five parts of a friendly letter?
14. What is the hardest part for you?

CHAPTER 15 LESSON 3 SKILL TEST B
(Student Page 129)

Exercise 1: In the numbered boxes below, write the six parts of a business letter.

Business Letter Parts

1.	2.	3.	5.
Box or street City, state, zip code Date	Name of Receiver Name of Company Box or street City, state, zip code	Dear Mr./Ms._____:	Sincerely yours,
		4. _____	6. Writer's Full Name

Exercise 2: Draw a line to separate all the parts and sentences of the business letter in the box below. Then, on notebook paper, use the information from the Business Letter Information Box to write a business letter in the correct form. Capitalize and punctuate as needed.

Business Letter Information Box

From: janette woods 578 hudson street white cloud michigan 82023 october 1 20____ dear mr hames i would like to order the blue deluxe sleeping bag #568 in your catalog enclosed is my check for $48.95 please send the sleeping bag by ups sincerely yours

To: robert c hames casey hunting supplies 1422 riverdale drive rifle colorado 79987

Exercise 3: In the numbered boxes below, write the two parts of an envelope used for a business letter.

Business Envelope Parts

1.	2.
Writer's Name Box or street City, state, zip code	Name of Receiver Name of Company Box or street City, state, zip code

Exercise 4: On your notebook paper, draw an envelope and use the parts in your Business Letter Information Box to help you address the envelope correctly. Also, draw a stamp on your envelope.

Exercise 5: Answer these questions about the business letter and envelope you have just completed.

1. Who wrote the letter?
2. Who will receive the letter?
3. When was the letter written?
4. Where does the writer live?
5. What closing did the writer use?
6. What greeting did this writer use?
7. What is another word for greeting?
8. What name is in the mailing address?
9. What name is in the return address?
10. Where does the person receiving the letter live?
11. What is this letter about?
12. Did you draw a stamp on the envelope?
13. What are the six parts of a business letter?
14. What is the hardest part for you?

CHAPTER 15 LESSON 4 APPLICATION TEST
(Student Page 130)

Exercise 1: Mixed Patterns 1-3. Classify each sentence.

1. _____ My teacher gave Jamie and Susan a big homework assignment over the holiday weekend.

2. _____ During vacation Maria and Lindsey climbed over the wall and sneaked into the concert.

3. _____ Did you send Victoria a box of candy for her birthday?

Directions: Complete the noun job table. Use Sentence 1.

List the Noun Used	List the Noun Job	Singular or Plural	Common or Proper
4.	5.	6.	7.
8.	9.	10.	11.
12.	13.	14.	15.
16.	17.	18.	19.
20.	21.	22.	23.

Exercise 2: Writing Assignment
Use the business letter situation given below to write a business letter. Then, draw a business letter envelope on the back of your business letter and fill in the mailing address and the return address. Put your finished writing in your Rough Draft folder.

Writing Assignment #22: Business Letter

Business Letter Situation: Read the advertisement below and select one pet you wish to order. Write a business letter, placing your order. Use your own mailing address. You will find all the information you need to order your pet if you read the ad very carefully.

LOVE-A-PET
Unusual Pets for Unusual Persons

Now you can own that VERY SPECIAL
UNUSUAL PET that you've never thought of before!

Select from these favorites
LLAMAS $75.00
COATI MUNDI $55.00
WOMBATS $45.00

And now for a limited time only
At the fantastically reduced rate of $7.50
GENUINE PIT VIPERS

Simply send the amount above plus only
$100 for shipping and handling to

LOVE-A-PET
3202 Everglade Trail
Swampland, FL 25000

CHAPTER 16 LESSON 3 APPLICATION TEST
(Student Page 141)

Exercise 1: Classify each sentence.

1. _____ After sunset the rain became sleet.

2. _____ The best mathematicians in our class are you and Beth.

3. _____ My uncle is a collector of rare art from Japan.

Directions: Complete the noun job table. Use Sentence 3.

List the Noun Used	List the Noun Job	Singular or Plural	Common or Proper
4.	5.	6.	7.
8.	9.	10.	11.
12.	13.	14.	15.
16.	17.	18.	19.

Exercise 2:
You are now going to combine your knowledge of persuasive writing and letter writing to write your second persuasive letter. Your second letter will be a **persuasive business letter**. It will have all the parts of a business letter in it; so, you must remember all you have learned about writing a business letter. The letter will also have some of the features of a persuasive essay; so, you must remember to consider the person whom you are trying to persuade.

Writing Assignment
Use the Steps for Writing a *Persuasive Business Letter* and the *Example Persuasive Business Letter* as you do the writing assignment below. Put your finished writing in your Rough Draft folder.

Writing Assignment #28: Use the persuasive business letter situation below.

Persuasive Business Letter Situation
Your assignment is to write a persuasive business letter on your own notebook paper. Without using Anne's idea of babysitting, come up with an idea for a business of your own. Use your own name and your own street address, city, state, and zip code. Use Ann's letter as a pattern and write a persuasive letter to Mr. Robert Blakemore, 856 Robin Cove. He lives in your hometown, so use your town and state to finish his address. Finally, draw and address an envelope for your letter, and don't forget to draw a stamp. **Letter and Envelope Information** To: Mr. Robert Blakemore, 856 Robin Cove, student's hometown, state, and zip From: Student's name, student's street address, student's city, state, and zip

CHAPTER 16 LESSON 4 SKILL TEST A
(Student Page 145)

Exercise 1: Number your paper from 1 to 7 and write the answer to each question.

1. What would you find by going to *The Readers' Guide to Periodical Literature*?
2. Name the main reference book that gives the definition, spelling, and pronunciation of words.
3. Name the main reference book that is primarily a book of maps.
4. Name the main reference book that is published once a year with a variety of up-to-date information.
5. How are fiction books arranged on the shelves?
6. How are nonfiction books arranged on the shelves?
7. What are the names of the three cards located in the card catalog?

Exercise 2: Number your paper from 8 to 14 and write the title and author of each fiction book below in the correct order to go on the shelves.

8. *Freckle Juice* by Judy Blume
9. *A Taste of Blueberries* by Doris Smith
10. *The Wise Fool* by Paul Galdone
11. *The Arrow of Fire* by Roy Snell
12. *Stone Soup* by Marcia Brown
13. *Good-bye My Island* by Jean Rogers
14. *Dirt Bike Racer* by Matt Christopher

Exercise 3: Number your paper from 15 to 22 and write True or False for each statement.

15. The card catalog is an index to books in the library.
16. The *Readers' Guide to Periodical Literature* is an index to magazines.
17. The title of the book is always the first line on each of the catalog cards.
18. The books in the fiction section are arranged alphabetically by the author's last name.
19. The books in the nonfiction section are arranged numerically by a call number.
20. Biographies are arranged on the shelves according to the author's last name.
21. Fiction and nonfiction books have numbers on their spines to locate them on a shelf.
22. Encyclopedias give concise information about persons, places, and events of world-wide interest.

Exercise 4: For 23-25, draw and label the three catalog cards for this book: 590.6 *Birds of All Kinds* by Walter Ferguson, Golden Press, N.Y., 1959, p.25. (Use the catalog card examples in Lesson 4.)

23. Author Card
24. Title Card
25. Subject Card

CHAPTER 16 LESSON 5 SKILL TEST B
(Student Page 147)

Exercise 1: Match each part of a book listed below with the type of information it may give you. Write the appropriate letter in the blank. You may use a letter more than once.

A. Title page	B. Table of contents	C. Copyright page	D. Index	E. Bibliography
F. Preface	G. Appendix	H. Glossary	I. Body	

1. _____ Illustrator's name

2. _____ Books for finding more information

3. _____ Titles of units and chapters

4. _____ Copyright date

5. _____ Publisher's name

6. _____ ISBN number

7. _____ Extra maps in a book

8. _____ Exact page numbers for a particular topic

9. _____ Author's name

10. _____ Text of the book

11. _____ Meanings of important words in the book

12. _____ Reason the book was written

13. _____ Used to locate topics quickly

14. _____ City where the book was published

15. _____ A list of books used by the author as references

Exercise 2: Name the five parts found at the front of a book.

16. _____
17. _____
18. _____
19. _____
20. _____

Exercise 3: Name the four parts found at the back of a book.

21. _____ 22. _____ 23. _____ 24. _____

CHAPTER 17 LESSON 5 APPLICATION TEST
(Student Page 166)

Exercise 1: Classify each sentence.

1. _____ During the rescue the firefighters became heroes in the eyes of the frightened families.

2. _____ Our favorite vacation place is the beach along the eastern coast of Florida.

3. _____ Fifteen tons of wheat will be an unusually large shipment for our small freight company.

Directions: Complete the noun job table. Use Sentence 3.

List the Noun Used	List the Noun Job	Singular or Plural	Common or Proper
4.	5.	6.	7.
8.	9.	10.	11.
12.	13.	14.	15.
16.	17.	18.	19.

Exercise 2: On notebook paper, write the correct answer to each question below.

20. List the 14 steps for researching a topic and writing a report.
21. Name the two kinds of outlines.
22. Name three sources you can use for a report.
23. Write the 5 things an outline must have.
24. Write the order of the pages of your report when they are handed in.

Exercise 3: Match the definitions. Write the correct number from the second column beside each concept in the first column.

_____ 25. a detailed list of the sources used in your report	1. parallel form
_____ 26. a card for each source used in your report	2. subtopics
_____ 27. reading the key parts to select a source	3. note cards
_____ 28. indicate the details in an outline	4. bibliography
_____ 29. give more information about a main topic	5. capital letters
_____ 30. file that lists all books in the library	6. title of source and page number
_____ 31. where to write notes	7. periodical
_____ 32. indicate main topics in an outline	8. sentence and topic
_____ 33. what to write at the top of each note card	9. main topics, subtopics, details
_____ 34. how notes are written	10. bibliography card
_____ 35. two kind of outlines	11. skimming
_____ 36. what to write at the bottom of a note card	12. in phrases, in your own words
_____ 37. parts of an outline	13. card catalog
_____ 38. outline parts should begin the same way	14. Roman numerals
_____ 39. indicate subtopics in an outline	15. a topic category
_____ 40. magazine	16. Arabic numerals

CHAPTER 18 LESSON 1 SKILL TEST
(Student Page 168)

Exercise 1: Write each underlined pronoun in the chart under **Pronoun**. Under **Job**, write **SP, OP, IO, DO,** or **PP** to tell its job in the sentence. Under **Case**, write **S** for the subjective case, **O** for the objective case, or **P** for the possessive case. Finally, write **S** for singular or **P** for plural. *(Use the letter C to signify compound jobs: COP)*

1. You (a) talked quietly on the phone about him (b).
2. She (c) skipped happily along the path to her (d) house.
3. He (e) sang sweetly for us (f) at the concert.
4. My (g) mom searched desperately for any information about him (h) and me (i).
5. We (j) boys gave Frank and him (k) a rod and reel set for their (l) birthday.

Pronoun	Job	Case (S, O, P)	S-P	Pronoun	Job	Case (S, O, P)	S-P
a.				g.			
b.				h.			
c.				i.			
d.				j.			
e.				k.			
f.				l.			

Exercise 2: Underline the correct pronoun choices. Then, write each pronoun job (**SP, OP, IO, DO, PP**) in the blank.

6. (She, Her) walked through the crowd with (he and I, him and me).	a.		b.
7. (He and I, Him and me) read loudly to (they, them).	c.		d.
8. (He, Him) cried sadly for (she and I, her and me).	e.		f.
9. (They, Them) worked quietly in the library with (us, we).	g.		h.
10. Paul and (her, she) invited (us, we) boys to the movies.	i.		j.

Exercise 3: Identify the point of view of each sentence by writing **1** for first, **2** for second, or **3** for third in each blank.

11. _____ I listened as the teacher spoke.　　14. _____ Jay and Mitch worked in their yard.

12. _____ Finish spreading the fertilizer.　　15. _____ They picked up rocks and planted grass.

13. _____ We are working in our yard.　　16. _____ You need to check this paper carefully.

Exercise 4: Identify the point of view of each paragraph as **1st, 2nd,** or **3rd** by putting parentheses around the number.

17.	Person: 1st 2nd 3rd	This is how you find the stadium. First, you travel north on Maple Street. Then, turn left on Oak Street and go 5 blocks. You will see the stadium on the right.
18.	Person: 1st 2nd 3rd	Patti and Jan like to sing songs with their children. They are always thinking of silly dances to go with the songs. They entertain the neighborhood with their funny songs and dances.
19.	Person: 1st 2nd 3rd	I often baby-sit for Sandy and Bill. I like to take their little girls to the park. We have fun on the swings and slides. Sometimes I pack my ice chest with a picnic lunch for us.

Exercise 5: Write personal pronouns in the blanks to make each paragraph the appropriate point-of-view.

20. 1st Person	(a) _____ enjoy watching old movies at (b) _____ house. (c) _____ like to eat popcorn while (d) _____ watch. (e) _____ favorite movies are the old Westerns that were popular when (f) _____ parents were young.
21. 3rd Person	John likes to play (a) _____ trombone loudly. (b) _____ family is proud of (c) _____; therefore, (d) _____ don't mind when (e) _____ practices loudly for long hours. (f) _____ just wear earplugs and keep smiling.

CHAPTER 18 LESSON 3 APPLICATION TEST
(Student Page 170)

Exercise 1: Mixed Patterns 1-4. Classify each sentence.

1. _____ Clothes, jewelry, and scarves were the items in her dresser drawer.

2. _____ Coach Hawkins is giving Tony and me lessons in wrestling after school.

3. _____ A flock of bewildered pigeons circled overhead during the electrical storm.

Exercise 2: Write each underlined pronoun in the chart under **Pronoun**. Under **Job**, write **SP**, **OP**, **IO**, **DO**, or **PP** to tell its job in the sentence. Under **Case**, write **S** for the subjective case, **O** for the objective case, or **P** for the possessive case. Finally, write **S** for singular or **P** for plural.

4. Our (a) new dog waits eagerly for us (b) in the afternoon.
5. He (c) barks at us (d) playfully in front of our (e) house.
6. We (f) play with him (g) every day after school in their (h) backyard.

Pronoun	Job	Case (S, O, P)	S-P	Pronoun	Job	Case (S, O, P)	S-P
a.				e.			
b.				f.			
c.				g.			
d.				h.			

Exercise 3: Underline the correct pronoun choices. Then, write each pronoun job **(SP, OP, IO, DO, PP)** in the blank.

7. (They, Them) waved at (him and me, he and I) from the window.	a.		b.
8. (She and I, Her and me) have spoken to the principal about (they, them).	c.		d.
9. (We, Us) girls baked (you, your) a cake yesterday.	e.		f.
10. (He and I, Him and Me) gave (they, them) tickets to the NCAA basketball tournament.	g.		h.

Exercise 4: Identify the point of view of each paragraph as **1st**, **2nd**, or **3rd** by putting parentheses around the number.

11.	Person: 1st 2nd 3rd	You learn how to be an effective speaker by following certain steps. First, you need to know your topic. Next, you organize your notes and practice. Finally, you look at your audience, smile, and begin.
12.	Person: 1st 2nd 3rd	Jim and I love early morning walks along the beach. We enjoy feeling the sand between our toes, and we enjoy watching the gentle morning waves sweep along the beach.
13.	Person: 1st 2nd 3rd	Toni and Jack looked at each other and laughed. They couldn't believe their luck! They had found their tickets to the game in Grumpy's doghouse!

Exercise 5: Editing Paragraph
Find each error and write the correction. Use the Editing Guide to help you. **Editing Guide: Capitals: 23 Commas: 6 Apostrophes: 5 A/An: 1 Misspelled Words: 2 Subject-Verb Agreement: 6 Quotations: 4 End Marks: 11**

the whole famile watch gleefully as dad turns on the tv to watch the basketball trounment soon dad leaps out of his easy chair and shout no that wasnt an foul get some glasses ref so that you can see the fouls then dad grab the remote control and switch the channel off the basketball game the quiet golf tournament doesnt help dads mood finally, he cant stand it any longer anxiously, dad switch back just as his favorite team the arkansas razorbacks shoots the winning basket oh no i cant believe i missed the whole thing dad moan

Note: The commas provided after the transition words *finally* and *anxiously* are not included in the total commas on the Editing Guide.

CHAPTER 19 LESSON 2 SKILL TEST A
(Student Page 177)

Exercise 1: Write the four demonstrative pronouns in the correct column in the chart below. Identify the underlined word as a demonstrative pronoun or adjective and as singular or plural by underlining the correct choices. If the underlined word is a pronoun, write its antecedent in the blank.

Singular, near	Plural, near	Singular, far	Plural, far
1.	2.	3.	4.

5. These new cars are on sale. (Pro, Adj) (Singular, Plural) _____
6. That is my first grade teacher in the blue dress. (Pro, Adj) (Singular, Plural) _____
7. This record player does not work properly. (Pro, Adj) (Singular, Plural) _____
8. Those are our lawn chairs there on the beach. (Pro, Adj) (Singular, Plural) _____
9. This is your science experiment on the table here. (Pro, Adj) (Singular, Plural) _____
10. That storm destroyed my garden last night. (Pro, Adj) (Singular, Plural) _____
11. These are the best paintings in the art show. (Pro, Adj) (Singular, Plural) _____
12. Those buildings are protected with fire insurance. (Pro, Adj) (Singular, Plural) _____

Exercise 2: In the first blank, write a demonstrative pronoun that agrees in number with its antecedent. In the second blank write the antecedent. Underline the correct verb that agrees in number with the subject.

13. _____ (is, are) the ladies in your club by the far door. _____

14. _____ (is, are) our classroom in here. _____

15. _____ (was, were) my sister's picture in the newspaper. _____

16. _____ (was, were) my favorite flowers in this entire garden! _____

Exercise 3: Tell whether the underlined word is an interrogative pronoun or adjective by underlining the **Int Pro** or the **Int Adj** in parentheses.

17. Which is the smallest piece of candy? (Int Pro, Int Adj)
18. Which programs are listed in the television magazine? (Int Pro, Int Adj)
19. Whose are those tickets on the table? (Int Pro, Int Adj)
20. Whose car keys are on the shelf by the door? (Int Pro, Int Adj)
21. What are your answers to my questions? (Int Pro, Int Adj)
22. What papers are lying all over the floor? (Int Pro, Int Adj)
23. Who has been invited to your party? (Int Pro, Int Adj)
24. Whom does the teacher help every day? (Int Pro, Int Adj)

Exercise 4: Underline the correct interrogative pronoun in the sentences below.

25. (Who, Whom) gave the order to advance?
26. The team was coached by (who, whom)?
27. (Who, Whom) did you see at the game?
28. To (who, whom) did you wish to speak?
29. Yesterday (who, whom) heard the shot?
30. (Who, Whom) did they select?

CHAPTER 19 LESSON 3 APPLICATION TEST
(Student Page 178)

Exercise 1: Classify each sentence.

1. _____ The adhesive tape was too sticky for the children.

2. _____ After the ceremony Sandra will be too tired for a shopping trip.

3. _____ My new boss was very tactful about the new rules and regulations on the job.

Directions: Complete the noun job table. Use Sentence 2.

List the Noun Used	List the Noun Job	Singular or Plural	Common or Proper
4.	5.	6.	7.
8.	9.	10.	11.
12.	13.	14.	15.

Exercise 2: Underline the demonstrative and interrogative words and then identify them by writing their abbreviations in the blank. (Use these abbreviations: **Dem Pro, Dem Adj, Int Pro, Int Adj**)

_____ 16. This is a fantastic view of the ocean!
_____ 17. That house burned to the ground on Christmas Eve.
_____ 18. What is the name of your school?
_____ 19. Which teams are picked for the exhibition game?
_____ 20. These file cabinets are full of tax records.
_____ 21. Who is the man in the white suit?
_____ 22. Whose sweater was left in the back of the room?
_____ 23. Those are the most colorful flowers in this show.
_____ 24. Whom did the judges name as the winner?
_____ 25. That is the science building over there.
_____ 26. These are the only books about Eisenhower in the library.
_____ 27. What time is the championship game on television?

Exercise 3: Underline the correct interrogative pronoun in the sentences below.

28. (Who, Whom) will you ask to the dance?
29. The plane was piloted by (who, whom)?
30. The chocolate pie was for (who, whom)?
31. Jim, (who, whom) was at the door?

Exercise 4: Editing Paragraph
Find each error and write the correction. Use the Editing Guide to help you. **Editing Guide: Capitals: 10   Commas: 7   Apostrophes: 4   Misspelled Words: 4   Quotations: 10   End Marks: 6**

rick rolled over and groaned sleepily as his sister came bouncing in his room early one spring morning time to get up for school she anounced cheerfully as she fliped on the lights and opened the blinds

janet moaned rick as he cautously opened one eye would you please tiptoe out the door after you turn the lights out and shut the blinds im so tired and its too early to get up

late night movies and early mornings dont mix chuckled janet then she added mischeivously lifes tough in the big city rick

CHAPTER 19 LESSON 5 SKILL TEST B
(Student Page 180)

Exercise 1: Write the four demonstrative pronouns in the correct column in the chart below. Identify the underlined word as a demonstrative pronoun or adjective and as singular or plural by underlining the correct choices. If the underlined word is a pronoun, write its antecedent in the blank.

Singular, near	Plural, near	Singular, far	Plural, far
1.	2.	3.	4.

5. <u>These</u> props are for our play. (Pro, Adj) (Singular, Plural) _____
6. <u>These</u> are the props for the play. (Pro, Adj) (Singular, Plural) _____
7. <u>That</u> was my favorite song on the radio. (Pro, Adj) (Singular, Plural) _____
8. <u>That</u> girl helps my aunt with her garden. (Pro, Adj) (Singular, Plural) _____
9. <u>Those</u> were Aunt Sophie's photographs. (Pro, Adj) (Singular, Plural) _____
10. <u>Those</u> pies tasted delicious yesterday. (Pro, Adj) (Singular, Plural) _____
11. <u>This</u> is the finest goldfish in the pond. (Pro, Adj) (Singular, Plural) _____
12. <u>This</u> watch is not keeping accurate time. (Pro, Adj) (Singular, Plural) _____

Exercise 2: In the first blank, write a demonstrative pronoun that agrees in number with its antecedent. In the second blank write the antecedent. Underline the correct verb that agrees in number with the subject.

13. _____ (is, are) Dad's muddy shoes on the porch. _____

14. _____ (is, are) our basketball team on the court. _____

15. _____ (was, were) Jenny's books over there. _____

16. _____ (was, were) an enjoyable evening. _____

Exercise 3: Tell whether the underlined word is an interrogative pronoun or adjective by underlining the **Int Pro** or the **Int Adj** in parentheses.

17. <u>Which</u> is the best costume for the contest? (Int Pro, Int Adj)
18. <u>Which</u> movie did you see at the theater? (Int Pro, Int Adj)
19. <u>Whose</u> coat is still hanging on the coat hook? (Int Pro, Int Adj)
20. <u>Whose</u> are those shoes? (Int Pro, Int Adj)
21. <u>What</u> subjects are offered at the community college? (Int Pro, Int Adj)
22. <u>What</u> is the name of the longest street in town? (Int Pro, Int Adj)
23. <u>Which</u> are the fish from the Gulf of Mexico? (Int Pro, Int Adj)
24. <u>Whose</u> are these computer discs? (Int Pro, Int Adj)

Exercise 4: Underline the correct interrogative pronoun in the sentences below.

25. (Who, Whom) did the announcer call?
26. The contest was won by (who, whom)?
27. (Who, Whom) does the crowd like best?
28. To (who, whom) does this mess belong?
29. (Who, Whom) solved the puzzle the fastest?
30. (Who, Whom) answered the doorbell just now?

CHAPTER 20 LESSON 1 SKILL TEST
(Student Page 183)

Exercise 1: Underline the correct personal pronoun once and underline its antecedent twice.

1. My cow had (her, their) calves in March.
2. Andrea made chicken for our guests. (She, They) enjoys cooking.
3. My ring fell through the boards on the deck. (It, They) were only two inches apart.
4. Linda found flower seeds for the garden. Jan helped her plant (it, them) in the ground.
5. Music and movies are very entertaining. (It, They) are my favorites!

Exercise 2: In the first column write **IP** or **Adj** to show if the underlined word is an indefinite pronoun or an adjective. In the second column write **SP, OP, DO, IO** to show the job of the indefinite pronoun. If the word is an adjective, write **Adj** in the second column.

IP or Adj		Pronoun Job/Adj
	6. Both of my parents enjoy mystery books.	
	7. Both shoes were covered with mud from the creek bed.	
	8. The telephone rang repeatedly for someone down the hall.	
	9. Everything was perfectly arranged in the display case.	
	10. Susan left everything on the table in the kitchen.	
	11. Several magazines were donated to the school library.	
	12. The company gave several of the employees a raise.	
	13. I did not hear from any of you over summer vacation.	
	14. Another child asked for permission first.	
	15. Everybody at the concert was singing with the choir.	

Exercise 3: For blanks 16-20, write five indefinite pronouns that are always plural. Then, for blanks 21-25, write five indefinite pronouns that are either singular or plural, depending on how they are used in the sentence.

16.	17.	18.	19.	20.
21.	22.	23.	24.	25.

Exercise 4: Underline each indefinite pronoun and write **S** or **P** for singular or plural in the blank. Then, underline the correct verb. Use the indefinite pronoun chart to help you.

26. ___ All of the cake (is, are) gone.
27. ___ None of the flowers (was, were) wilted.
28. ___ All of the students (is, are) here.
29. ___ Most of the bread (has, have) mold on it.
30. ___ Most of the people (has, have) a job.
31. ___ Everyone with tickets (were, was) admitted.
32. ___ Several of my dogs (is, are) hungry.
33. ___ One of the tables (is, are) broken.
34. ___ Few of the guests (has, have) a bobsled.
35. ___ Several in this box (is, are) torn.
36. ___ Each of the cars (has, have) a big price tag.
37. ___ Few in our class (has, have) failed.
38. ___ Neither of the dresses (interest, interests) me.
39. ___ Some of the milk (is, are) sour.
40. ___ None of the material (was, were) wasted.
41. ___ Some of the grapes (is, are) sour.
42. ___ All of my work (is, are) finished.
43. ___ Some of the glare (has, have) disappeared.
44. ___ Everyone in the audience (is, are) clapping.
45. ___ Both of the pies (is, are) apple.
46. ___ Somebody (know, knows) the answer.
47. ___ Everything on the tables (is, are) delicious.
48. ___ Someone in the stands (is, are) waving at us.
49. ___ Nobody (know, knows) our phone number.
50. ___ Both of the trees (is, are) old.
51. ___ No one in the crowd (look, looks) familiar.

Level 7 Skill and Application Test Workbook

CHAPTER 20 LESSON 3 APPLICATION TEST A
(Student Page 187)

Exercise 1: Classify each sentence.

1. _____ Mrs. Gruff was exceedingly angry with the four boys and their obnoxious dogs.

2. _____ Mark and Dewayne are extremely intelligent.

3. _____ The dogs in the fenced yard seemed unusually happy and playful at the approach of the boys.

Directions: Complete the noun job table. Use Sentence 3.

List the Noun Used	List the Noun Job	Singular or Plural	Common or Proper
4.	5.	6.	7.
8.	9.	10.	11.
12.	13.	14.	15.
16.	17.	18.	19.

Exercise 2: Draw one line under the subject and write **S** or **P** for singular or plural in the blank. Then, underline the correct verb and the correct possessive pronoun to agree with the subject. Use the Indefinite Pronoun Chart to help you.

20. _____ The flowers (loses, lose) (its, their) petals in the strong wind.
21. _____ Many of the boys (competes, compete) in (his, their) division.
22. _____ Neither of the women (like, likes) (her, their) dessert.
23. _____ Tom and Sally (goes, go) to town in (his, her, their) convertible.
24. _____ Each member of the girls' team (earn, earns) (her, their) own letter.
25. _____ Each of the girls in the contest (try, tries) (her, their) best.
26. _____ Did every member (pays, pay) (their, his) dues?
27. _____ The crowd (wave, waves) (their, its) flags and (yells, yell).
28. _____ Everyone in the club (supports, support) (his, their) team.
29. _____ (Don't, Doesn't) all of the animals in the zoo have (its, their) good points?
30. _____ Everyone (clap, claps) (his, their) hands at the pep rally.
31. _____ Few in the audience (want, wants) (his, their) names announced.
32. _____ Each of the soldiers (run, runs) twenty miles a day in (his, their) unit.

Exercise 3: In the first column write **IP** or **Adj** to show if the underlined word is an indefinite pronoun or an adjective. In the second column write **SP, OP, DO, IO** to show the job of the indefinite pronoun. If the word is an adjective, write **Adj** in the second column.

IP or Adj		Pronoun Job/Adj
	33. Many waited patiently in line for their tickets.	
	34. He wanted a few of the seashells on the beach.	
	35. Several packages arrived in the mail.	
	36. Dad gave somebody a call on the phone.	
	37. Susan left hurriedly with everything in her hands.	

Exercise 4: Underline each indefinite pronoun and write **S** or **P** for singular or plural in the blank. Underline the correct verb and the correct possessive pronoun to agree with the subject. Use the Indefinite Pronoun Chart to help you.

38. _____ Nobody (take, takes) (his, their) break at this time.
39. _____ Few (has, have) computers in (her, their) homes.
40. _____ Either of the answers (is, are) correct.
41. _____ Any of these books (is, are) available to the public.

CHAPTER 20 LESSON 3 APPLICATION TEST B
(Student Page 188)

Exercise 5: Review! Underline the correct pronoun choice in each sentence.

1. Between you and (I, me), there's nothing to do.
2. The money was divided between Mr. Jones and (he, him).
3. (We, Us) designers have interesting work.
4. Sam asked (we, us) boys to be present.
5. (We, Us) programmers deserve a raise.
6. Linda and (her, she) will bring dessert.
7. Are you going with Anna and (her, she)?
8. (Him and me)(He and I) are radio hams.
9. That solution seems beyond Charlie and (him, he).
10. Larry, Jason, and (me, I) are studying for our chemistry test.
11. The scoutmaster saw that everyone had (his, their) shoes on.
12. Everybody expected to hear (his, their) name called.
13. It was (us, we).
14. This is (him, he).
15. This is (her, she).
16. Have you any news for (us, we) girls?
17. (We, Us) members are going to have a meeting.

Exercise 6: Write an indefinite pronoun in the blank. Make sure it agrees with the verb and possessive pronoun in number.

18. _____ of the money sits in a vault in the bank. (*must be singular*)

19. _____ concentrates on her own project. (*must be singular*)

20. _____ of the students were painting murals. (*must be plural*)

21. _____ from the school has joined the debate team. (*must be singular*)

Exercise 7:   Editing Paragraph
Find each error and write the correction. Replace words underlined once with a synonym. Use the Editing Guide to help you. **Editing Guide: Synonyms: 1 Capitals: 22 Commas: 3 Periods: 3 Apostrophes: 3 Misspelled Words: 5 Subject-Verb Agreement: 2 Pronoun Usage: 4 End Marks: 9**

my friends and me love to make hard candy for our christmas carnivel hard candy is easy to make and fun to eat us girls get together on the first saturday of december at lindas house on oak street in canton ohio to make our carnivel candy we makes hard candy by boiling suger and corn syup until it forms a <u>heavy</u> syrup us girls then add flavors and coloring to the syrup then we make the syrup into shapes while it is still worm when its cool it is hard candy everyone tell we girls what a good job we do after last years carnivel mr j c simpson said that we girls should also make cream candy to sell next year

Exercise 8: Identify each complete sentence below by putting a slash between each sentence. Then, rewrite the paragraph on your notebook paper. Correct fragments and improve sentences by using a combination of simple, compound, and complex sentences. Underline simple sentences once, compound sentences twice, and put parentheses around the complex sentences.

Larry is going to camp this summer and Joe is going too and I am going with them and we are going with Boy Scout Troop 14 and we are going on a Greyhound bus and our camp is called Camp Evergreen and Camp Evergreen is located north of Bird Lake and Bird Lake is located near Benson, Minnesota and lots of swimming and fishing and are excited about our trip

CHAPTER 21 LESSON 1 SKILL TEST
(Student Page 193)

Exercise 1: Identify each set of pronouns in the box below by writing these abbreviations in the column labeled *Pro Name*: **D** for demonstrative pronouns, **I** for indefinite pronouns, **Int** for interrogative pronouns, and **P** for personal pronouns. Write **S** or **P** for singular or plural in the **S** or **P** column. If the pronouns can be either singular or plural, write **S,P** in the blank. Also, identify *personal pronouns* in the last two columns according to person (1st, 2nd, or 3rd) and case (**S**-subjective, **P**-possessive, or **O**-objective).

	Pronoun Identification Box				
	Pro Name			For personal pronouns only	
	D, I, Int, P	S or P		Person: 1, 2, 3	Case: S, P, O
1.			us, you, them		
2.			neither, no one, one		
3.			anybody, anyone, anything		
4.			me, you, him, her, it		
5.			nothing, nobody		
6.			it, its		
7.			he, him, his		
8.			everything, everybody, everyone		
9.			my, his, her, your, its		
10.			this, that		
11.			she, her, hers		
12.			both, few, many, several, others		
13.			we, us, our, ours		
14.			these, those		
15.			another, each, either		
16.			they, them, their, theirs		
17.			I, you, he, she, it		
18.			I, me, my, mine		
19.			you, your, yours		
20.			all, some, none		
21.			you, your, yours		
22.			you, we, they		
23.			our, your, their		
24.			most, any		

Write the five interrogative pronouns.

25.	26.	27.	28.	29.

CHAPTER 21 LESSON 3 APPLICATION TEST A
(Student Page 194)

Exercise 1: Mixed Patterns 1-5. Classify each sentence.

1. _____ Will the pleasant professor finally proceed with the history lesson?

2. _____ The governor and his secretary had a thorough knowledge of the government of Great Britain and the United States.

3. _____ Read Sally and me a bedtime story tonight.

4. _____ That old Ford is an antique car.

Directions: Complete the noun job table. Use Sentence 4.

List the Noun Used	List the Noun Job	Singular or Plural	Common or Proper
5.	6.	7.	8.
9.	10.	11.	12.

Exercise 2: Complete the chart below by writing these eight pronouns in the correct column: *they, him, her, who, this, everyone, both, these.*

Demonstrative Pronouns		Indefinite Pronouns		Interrogative Pronoun	Personal Pronouns		
Singular	Plural	Singular	Plural		Subjective	Possessive	Objective

Exercise 3:   **Editing Paragraph**
Find each error and write the correction. Use the Editing Guide to help you. **Editing Guide: Homonyms:** 1 **Capitals:** 14
Commas: 1 **Periods:** 4 **Apostrophes:** 2 **Misspelled Words:** 7 **Colons:** 3 **End Marks:** 8

dave turned sixteen at 8 05 a m on tuesday morning and he walked eagerly into the texas state revenue office at 8 10 to take his driving test he passed the written test with flying colors and waited confidently for his turn to test-drive with the state trooper the sober-faced policeman gave him a passing certificate and sent him inside the revenue office to get his license

dave walked slowly out of the revene office at 5 10 p m on tuesday afternoon without his license he liked sadly at all the papers in his hand and remebered the long waiting lines and all the clerks behind eight diferent windows he still couldnt beleive how many times he had stood in line at the wrong window he hoped he could get in line early enough tomorrow morning too finally get his drivers license he sighed again as he put a quater in the pay phone and called his mom to come drive him home

CHAPTER 21 LESSON 3 APPLICATION TEST B
(Student Page 195)

Exercise 4: Identify each set of pronouns in the box below by writing these abbreviations in the column labeled *Pro Name*: **D** for demonstrative pronouns, **I** for indefinite pronouns, **Int** for interrogative pronouns, and **P** for personal pronouns. Write **S** or **P** for singular or plural in the *S* or *P* column. If the pronouns can be either singular or plural, write **S,P** in the blank. Also, identify *personal pronouns* in the last two columns according to person (1st, 2nd, or 3rd) **AND** case (**S**-subjective, **P**-possessive, or **O**-objective). **Personal pronouns must have answers for both person and case.**

	Pronoun Identification Box				
	Pro Name			For personal pronouns only	
	D, I, Int, P	S or P		Person: 1, 2, 3	Case: S, P, O
1.			anybody		
2.			we		
3.			these		
4.			each		
5.			him		
6.			both		
7.			I		
8.			this		
9.			anything		
10.			our		
11.			me		
12.			neither		
13.			it		
14.			you		
15.			my		
16.			some		
17.			your		
18.			they		
19.			any		
20.			us		
21.			her		
22.			either		
23.			his		
24.			hers		
25.			that		
26.			their		
27.			everybody		
28.			mine		
29.			none		
30.			those		
31.			few		

Write the five interrogative pronouns.

32.	33.	34.	35.	36.

Exercise 5: Underline the correct pronoun for the sentences below.

37. Larry showed (she, her) and Ted his car.
38. (Who, Whom) did Sue visit?
39. The coach gave Bob and (I, me) an award.
40. This is (he, him).

Level 7 Skill and Application Test Workbook

CHAPTER 22 LESSON 1 SKILL TEST
(Student Page 201)

Exercise 1: Write the correct contraction beside these words.

1. is not _____
2. you have _____
3. there is _____
4. they will _____
5. we would _____
6. I am _____
7. does not _____
8. they had _____
9. we have _____
10. let us _____
11. has not _____
12. she has _____
13. you will _____
14. were not _____
15. cannot _____

Exercise 2: Write the correct words beside each contraction.

16. he'll _____
17. don't _____
18. hasn't _____
19. I've _____
20. they'd _____
21. we've _____
22. they're _____
23. you're _____
24. who's _____
25. it's _____
26. aren't _____
27. it's _____
28. I'll _____
29. I'd _____
30. she'd _____

Exercise 3: Underline the correct contraction or possessive pronoun for each sentence.

31. (Your, You're) going to the mall in (your, you're) car today.
32. (Whose, Who's) the guest speaker tonight?
33. (Their, They're) sure (their, they're) books were stolen?
34. (Whose, Who's) is the best apple pie in the baking contest?
35. (Its, It's) finally time to celebrate because the class receives (its, it's) award.
36. (Your, You're) sure that (their, they're) still here?

Exercise 4: Write a reflexive or intensive pronoun in the first blank and write **R** or **I** in the second blank to identify the pronoun as reflexive or intensive.

1. The instructors _____ missed their early class. _____

2. Dad chuckled to _____ during the play. _____

3. The old rifle _____ was in excellent condition. _____

4. The young army cook gave _____ an extra helping. _____

Exercise 5: Underline the correct contraction or possessive pronoun for each sentence.

Larry and Jerry are the best players on (your, you're) football team. (They're, Their) talent and hard work are admired by everyone in town. (Its, It's) fun to watch them play ball. (They're, Their) always running touchdowns. (Its, It's) no secret (whose, who's) team will win the conference.

Exercise 6: Write a paragraph on your notebook paper using and underlining contractions and possessive pronouns.

CHAPTER 22 LESSON 3 APPLICATION TEST A
(Student Page 203)

Exercise 1: Mixed Patterns 6-7. Classify each sentence.

1. _____ Bad TV habits can make a person lazy.

2. _____ The committee named Elizabeth head of the litter campaign.

3. _____ The judges declared Polly the winner of the skating competition.

4. _____ No one in the kindergarten class colored his pumpkin orange!

Directions: Complete the noun job table. Use Sentence 2.

List the Noun Used	List the Noun Job	Singular or Plural	Common or Proper
5.	6.	7.	8.
9.	10.	11.	12.
13.	14.	15.	16.
17.	18.	19.	20.

Exercise 2: Complete the chart below by writing these seven pronouns in the correct column: *anybody, that, we, us, few ours, what.*

Demonstrative Pronouns		Indefinite Pronouns		Interrogative Pronoun	Personal Pronouns		
Singular	Plural	Singular	Plural		Subjective	Possessive	Objective

Exercise 3: Underline the correct contraction or possessive pronoun for each sentence.

1. (You're, Your) parents said that (you're, your) leaving for Utah on Sunday.
2. (They're, Their) working outside in (they're, their) backyard on the pool.
3. (Who's, Whose) watching the house while (you're, your) in Europe on (you're, your) vacation?
4. (It's, Its) too bad (they're, their) late for the concert.

Exercise 4: Punctuate the quotations and capitalize words as needed.

5. yummy exclaimed harold that chocolate cake looks delicious
6. jerry arent your parents picking you up after the game asked amanda

Exercise 5:   Editing Paragraph
Find each error and write the correction. Use the Editing Guide to help you. **Editing Guide: Homonyms: 1   Capitals: 18   Commas: 5   Periods: 2   Misspelled Words: 4   End Marks: 6**

the small boy eyed his mom in dispair ms smith his latin teacher had been talking to his mom

for ten minutes he knew his grades in biology I and calculus II were excellant his grades in latin class

had droped just a little but they were still good sudenly his mom winked at him said good bye to

ms smith and motioned for him to sit beside her she lovingly reminded her son that he was only ten

years old and had to more years before he entered the venus technical college for advanced aerodynamics

CHAPTER 22 LESSON 3 APPLICATION TEST B
(Student Page 204)

Exercise 6: Write the correct contraction beside these words.

1. it is _____
2. there is _____
3. is not _____
4. you have _____
5. they will _____
6. will not _____
7. you have _____
8. let us _____
9. he will _____
10. I am _____
11. I will _____
12. you will _____
13. was not _____
14. do not _____
15. they have _____
16. we would _____
17. have not _____
18. does not _____

Exercise 7: Write the correct words beside each contraction.

19. you're _____
20. they're _____
21. he's _____
22. they'd _____
23. he'll _____
24. we'd _____
25. I've _____
26. don't _____
27. we've _____
28. hasn't _____
29. who's _____
30. I'm _____
31. they're _____
32. you'd _____
33. it's _____
34. wasn't _____

Exercise 8: Write a reflexive or intensive pronoun in the first blank and write **R** or **I** in the second blank to identify the pronoun as reflexive or intensive.

35. The phone _____ was working perfectly. _____

36. My older sister looked at _____ in the mirror. _____

37. My friends built _____ a sand castle on the beach. _____

38. I _____ enjoyed the banquet very much. _____

39. Randy painted the car _____. _____

Exercise 9: Underline the correct pronoun choice.

40. Sandy and (I, me) were packing for our trip to the mountains.
41. You and (he, him) have eaten too much.
42. Mother frowned at Linda and (I, me).
43. (Us, we) boys are going camping this weekend.
44. Adam and (he, him) are the class clowns.
45. Lindsay talked to Mom and (I, me) about the trip.
46. The storm caught Dad and (I, me) inside the store.

CHAPTER 23 LESSON 1 SKILL TEST
(Student Page 208)

Exercise 1: Write the correct contraction beside these words.

1. he is _____	6. I am _____	11. I had _____
2. you have _____	7. was not _____	12. does not _____
3. you had _____	8. do not _____	13. they had _____
4. you will _____	9. had not _____	14. we have _____
5. you would _____	10. let us _____	15. I have _____

Exercise 2: Write the correct words beside each contraction.

16. didn't _____	21. he'd _____	26. I'm _____
17. they'd _____	22. they're _____	27. aren't _____
18. hasn't _____	23. you're _____	28. you'd _____
19. I've _____	24. who's _____	29. you've _____
20. he's _____	25. it's _____	30. let's _____

Exercise 3: Underline the appositive in each sentence and put the commas where they belong.

31. Fred hid in the shack an old deserted beach bungalow.
32. The crew of the shuttle saw the lights bright stars in the sky.
33. John the lawyer on the case presented the winning argument.
34. Mary dug a hole a tiny cavity in the front lawn.
35. Bethany proudly drove the red car a Lexus to the bank for a loan.
36. The koala a lover of eucalyptus leaves is a native of Australia.
37. The naturalist gave the birds two orioles plenty of birdseed during the winter months.
38. The monk walked to the monastery door a massive wooden frame and entered the long hall.
39. Will Henry our leader be open to that suggestion?
40. Take your lunch two sandwiches and an orange and go to the park.

Exercise 4: Write a reflexive or intensive pronoun in the first blank and write **R** or **I** in the second blank to identify the pronoun as reflexive or intensive.

41. My brother laughed at _____ when his trick backfired. _____

42. The students _____ supervised the halls. _____

43. The funny circus clown gave _____ a round of applause. _____

44. My father said that the motorcycle _____ was a piece of junk. _____

CHAPTER 23 LESSON 3 APPLICATION TEST
(Student Page 210)

Exercise 1: Classify each sentence.

1. _____ My sister gleefully painted the wall orange.

2. _____ The cheerleaders named little Amy their cheerleading mascot.

3. _____ Did the teacher believe Julius Caesar a villain?

Directions: Complete the noun job table. Use Sentence 1.

List the Noun Used	List the Noun Job	Singular or Plural	Common or Proper
4.	5.	6.	7.
8.	9.	10.	11.

Exercise 2: Complete the chart below by writing these seven pronouns in the correct column: *another, those, whom, I, her, its, others*.

Demonstrative Pronouns		Indefinite Pronouns		Interrogative Pronoun	Personal Pronouns		
Singular	Plural	Singular	Plural		Subjective	Possessive	Objective

Exercise 3: Underline the correct contraction or possessive pronoun for each sentence.

1. "(You're, Your) a lucky boy," she said. "I am happy to present (you're, your) award!"
2. (They're, Their) yelling and waving (they're, their) arms at the bus driver!
3. (Who's, Whose) umbrella is on the kitchen table?
4. (It's, Its) feet are too big for (it's, its) body.

Exercise 4: Underline the appositive in each sentence and put the commas where they belong.

5. After the storm last night Julia found two damaged trees a pine and a cedar.
6. The lamp an antique oil model hung on Uncle Bertram's den wall.
7. Jerome yelled for his soccer team an exciting group of players.
8. Above the clouds thick cumulous billows the dark birds flew.
9. Hazel a rabbit in *Watership Down* becomes the chief rabbit.

Exercise 5:   **Editing Paragraph**
Find each error and write the correction. Use the Editing Guide to help you. **Editing Guide: Homonyms: 2   Capitals: 15   Commas: 6   A/An: 1   Misspelled Words: 4   End Marks: 7**

    everyone began gathering at dawn in the parking lot of northside jounior high school excited seventh graders greeted friends and carried dufel bags and pillows to there buses anxious parents gave last minute instructions to chaprones busy teachers worked hard too keep children parents chaperones and belongings organized finally everything was ready for departur as the buses pulled away happy students waved at sleepy parents already dreaming of their beds at home the seventh graders and an few brave adults were going to space camp in huntsville alabama

CHAPTER 24 LESSON 1 SKILL TEST A
(Student Page 216)

Exercise 1: Fill in the helping verb chart.

Future Tense	Present Perfect Tense		Past Perfect Tense	Future Perfect Tense
2 verbs	Singular-1	Plural-1	1 verb	3 verbs

Exercise 2: Underline each verb or verb phrase. In the first column, identify the verb tense by writing its corresponding number in the blank from the following list: (1) Present Tense (2) Past Tense (3) Future Tense (4) Present Perfect Tense (5) Past Perfect Tense (6) Future Perfect Tense. Then, in the second column, write **R** or **I** for Regular or Irregular.

Verb Tense	R or I

1. They frequently talk about current events in that class.
2. Raymond talked on the phone for several minutes.
3. My parents will talk to your parents about our trip.
4. These office machines run all day on a small amount of electricity.
5. My Uncle Ray ran for mayor last November.
6. Our men's club will run in the Boston Marathon next month.
7. Joanne has talked to the salesperson for over an hour.
8. The contestants had answered every question within the time limit.
9. By tonight the children will have opened their presents.
10. Aunt Pat and her family have always sung at our family reunions.

Exercise 3: Conjugate the verb *begin* in the chart below.

Conjugation of the Verb *Begin*					
Present	Past	Future	Present Perfect	Past Perfect	Future Perfect
(No helping verbs)	(No helping verbs)	(will or shall)	(has or have)	(had)	(will/shall) + have
Singular / Plural					

Exercise 4: Conjugate the verb *work* in the chart below.

Conjugation of the Verb *Work*					
Present	Past	Future	Present Perfect	Past Perfect	Future Perfect
(No helping verbs)	(No helping verbs)	(will or shall)	(has or have)	(had)	(will/shall) + have
Singular / Plural					

CHAPTER 24 LESSON 2 SKILL TEST B
(Student Page 220)

Test Exercise 1: Conjugation of the Verb *Look*

Write the names of the four principal parts:

Present		Past	Future	Present Perfect	Past Perfect	Future Perfect
(No helping verbs)		(No helping verbs)	(will or shall)	(has or have)	(had)	(will/shall) + have
Singular	Plural					

Simple Progressive Forms			Perfect Progressive Forms			Simple Emphatic	
am/is/are	was/were	will/shall + be	has/have + been	had + been	will/shall + have been	do/does	did

Test Exercise 2: Conjugation of the Verb *Talk*

Present		Past	Future	Present Perfect	Past Perfect	Future Perfect
(No helping verbs)		(No helping verbs)	(will or shall)	(has or have)	(had)	(will/shall) + have
Singular	Plural					

Simple Progressive Forms			Perfect Progressive Forms			Simple Emphatic	
am/is/are	was/were	will/shall + be	has/have + been	had + been	will/shall + have been	do/does	did

Test Exercise 3: Conjugation of the Verb *Sink*

Present		Past	Future	Present Perfect	Past Perfect	Future Perfect
(No helping verbs)		(No helping verbs)	(will or shall)	(has or have)	(had)	(will/shall) + have
Singular	Plural					

Simple Progressive Forms			Perfect Progressive Forms			Simple Emphatic	
am/is/are	was/were	will/shall + be	has/have + been	had + been	will/shall + have been	do/does	did

Test Exercise 4: Conjugate the verb *fly* on your paper.

CHAPTER 24 LESSON 2 SKILL TEST C
(Student Page 221)

Exercise 1: Fill in the helping verb chart.

Future Tense	Present Perfect		Past Perfect	Future Perfect	Progressive Form		Emphatic Form	
2 verbs	Singular-1	Plural-1	1 verb	3 verbs	Singular-5	Plural-4	Singular-2	Plural-2

Exercise 2: Underline each verb or verb phrase. In the first column, identify the verb tense by writing its corresponding number in the blank from the following list: (1) Present Tense (2) Past Tense (3) Future Tense (4) Present Perfect Tense (5) Past Perfect Tense (6) Future Perfect Tense (7) Progressive Form (8) Emphatic Form. Then, in the second column, write **R** or **I** for Regular or Irregular. (*Progressive and emphatic verbs are identified by form without noting the tense.*)

Verb Tense	R or I

1. The army helicopter had landed safely on the landing pad.
2. A flock of geese is landing on the lake behind our house.
3. The successful actor's chauffeur will drive him to the awards ceremony.
4. The eager children watch expectantly for signs of the first snow.
5. The excited second grader did find a quarter on the playground.
6. Dad and Grandpa will have slept for eight hours by now.
7. Three happy toddlers were splashing in the wading pool.
8. Our committee had been deciding the best theme for the dance.
9. You did an excellent job on your science project this year.
10. A freight company will have moved our furniture to Utah by next week.
11. The grouchy woman grumbled under her breath about the weather.
12. The young doctor is an expert on diseases of the skin.
13. The company boss will raise your salary at the end of the year.
14. Mrs. Sanders has been driving our school bus for fifteen years.
15. The door to the baby's room does creak loudly on its hinges.

Exercise 3: Conjugate the verb *see* in the chart below.

Conjugation of the Verb *See*					
Write the names of the four principal parts:					
Present	**Past**	**Future**	**Present Perfect**	**Past Perfect**	**Future Perfect**
(No helping verbs)	(No helping verbs)	(will or shall)	(has or have)	(had)	(will/shall) + have
Singular Plural					

Simple Progressive Forms			Perfect Progressive Forms			Simple Emphatic	
am/is/are	was/were	will/shall + be	has/have + been	had + been	will/shall + have been	do/does	did

CHAPTER 24 LESSON 3 SKILL TEST D
(Student Page 222)

Exercise 1: Fill in the helping verb chart.

Future Tense	Present Perfect		Past Perfect	Future Perfect	Progressive Form		Emphatic Form	
2 verbs	Singular-1	Plural-1	1 verb	3 verbs	Singular-5	Plural-4	Singular-2	Plural-2

Exercise 2: Underline each verb or verb phrase. In the first column, identify the verb tense by writing its corresponding number in the blank from the following list: (1) Present Tense (2) Past Tense (3) Future Tense (4) Present Perfect Tense (5) Past Perfect Tense (6) Future Perfect Tense (7) Progressive Form (8) Emphatic Form. Then, in the second column, write **R** or **I** for Regular or Irregular. *(Progressive and emphatic verbs are identified by form without noting the tense.)*

Verb Tense	R or I

1. My Aunt Molly bakes her lasagna for one hour.
2. The girls had eaten at the Chinese restaurant for lunch.
3. The judges did choose a beautiful girl as the winner.
4. The skilled surgeons will operate on several heart patients this morning.
5. The small child's balloon had burst into tiny pieces.
6. The drama club will be performing this afternoon for our class.
7. The campaign workers have been telling everyone about their candidate.
8. Those trained soldiers do shoot accurately under pressure.
9. Our neighbors planted flowers and bushes in their front yard.
10. By this time tomorrow morning, we will have driven 500 miles on our trip.
11. That old truck has pulled many disabled vehicles in the last ten years.
12. The children in the hospital will have been laughing at the silly clown.
13. My grandmother does a good job at the bakery.
14. My grandfather was a pilot during the Korean War.
15. Government officials are considering a compromise of their trade policies.

Exercise 3: Conjugate the verb *hop* in the chart below.

Conjugation of the Verb *Hop*						
Write the names of the four principal parts:						
Present		Past	Future	Present Perfect	Past Perfect	Future Perfect
(No helping verbs)		(No helping verbs)	(will or shall)	(has or have)	(had)	(will/shall) + have
Singular	Plural					

Simple Progressive Forms			Perfect Progressive Forms			Simple Emphatic	
am/is/are	was/were	will/shall + be	has/have + been	had + been	will/shall + have been	do/does	did

CHAPTER 24 LESSON 4 SKILL TEST E
(Student Page 223)

Exercise 1: Fill in the helping verb chart.

Future Tense	Present Perfect		Past Perfect	Future Perfect	Progressive Form		Emphatic Form	
2 verbs	Singular-1	Plural-1	1 verb	3 verbs	Singular -5	Plural - 4	Singular-2	Plural-2

Exercise 2: Underline each verb or verb phrase. In the first column, identify the verb tense by writing its corresponding number in the blank from the following list: (1) Present Tense (2) Past Tense (3) Future Tense (4) Present Perfect Tense (5) Past Perfect Tense (6) Future Perfect Tense (7) Progressive Form (8) Emphatic Form. Then, in the second column, write **R** or **I** for Regular or Irregular. *(Progressive and emphatic verbs are identified by form without noting the tense.)*

Verb Tense	R or I

1. This medicine will prevent minor ailments during your trip.
2. After tonight, the tiny infant will have slept in her crib only twice.
3. I open the mail every day with a letter opener.
4. All students will be using this textbook for the coming year.
5. The caterpillar had become a butterfly through metamorphosis.
6. We will have walked five miles at the end of the course.
7. The innocent rabbit didn't see the fox behind the bushes.
8. The players finished the game after three extra innings.
9. The golf team had been playing at the country club last week.
10. That row of children will move at the proper time after the play.
11. My math teacher erased the answers from the board!
12. Our dog Bozo does like our cat Bingo most of the time.
13. The electric company will be sending a refund check soon.
14. The security guards have closed these doors for a reason.
15. Mom drinks coffee with cream every morning at breakfast.

Exercise 3: Conjugate the verb *drive* in the chart below.

Conjugation of the Verb *Drive*					
Write the names of the four principal parts:					
Present	**Past**	**Future**	**Present Perfect**	**Past Perfect**	**Future Perfect**
(No helping verbs)	(No helping verbs)	(will or shall)	(has or have)	(had)	(will/shall) + have
Singular Plural					

Simple Progressive Forms			Perfect Progressive Forms			Simple Emphatic	
am/is/are	was/were	will/shall + be	has/have + been	had + been	will/shall + have been	do/does	did

CHAPTER 24 LESSON 5 POSTTEST
(Student Page 224)

Exercise 1: Classify each sentence.

1. _____ Several plump robins searched diligently for juicy worms in my back yard.

2. _____ For my birthday my generous parents gave me the most important item on my list.

3. _____ Quickly, Jocelyn and her little brother led the five horses into the barn.

4. _____ Four very excited fans were irate after the referee's call!

5. _____ Can that history teacher make this class interesting to his students?

6. _____ My two cousins in El Paso are students at Coronado High School.

7. _____ After an exciting election, John Conner named Sarah Warren chairman of the committee.

Exercise 2: Identify each pronoun as indefinite or personal **(I, P)** and as singular or plural **(S, P)**. Underline your choices.

8. we   (I or P) (S or P)   10. everybody (I or P) (S or P)   12. she   (I or P) (S or P)   14. both (I or P) (S or P)
9. each (I or P) (S or P)   11. they   (I or P) (S or P)   13. either (I or P) (S or P)   15. it   (I or P) (S or P)

Exercise 3: Identify each verb as regular or irregular and put **R** or **I** in the blank. Then, write the past tense form.

16. cook _____ _____   17. swim _____ _____   18. break _____ _____

Exercise 4: Fill in the helping verb chart and name the four principal parts of a verb.

19. Write the names of the four principal parts:

Future Tense	Present Perfect		Past Perfect	Future Perfect	Progressive Form		Emphatic Form	
2 verbs	Singular-1	Plural-1	1 verb	3 verbs	Singular -5	Plural - 4	Singular-2	Plural-2

Exercise 5: Correct the errors in the following paragraph. Replace words underlined once with a synonym and words underlined twice with an antonym. Use this editing guide: **Capitals: 27 Homonyms: 6 End Marks: 7 Commas: 4 Semicolons: 1 Subject-Verb Agreement: 4 Apostrophes: 2 Synonym: 3 Antonym: 1 Spelling: 2**

during march my whole family enjoy watching the n c a a division 1 national mens basketball tournament we each <u>choose</u> the too teams we think will make the finals susan and dad <u>always</u> picks u c l a as one of there teams last year some of the games was in kansas city kansas which is near our home sense the games was so close we went two one session and saw for <u>excellent</u> games my <u>dream</u> is to play collage basketball however i am to short i guess ill just have to consintrate on growing

Student Posttest Response Sheet

Write at least a paragraph explaining the benefits of having good English skills.

CHAPTER 25 LESSON 1

Changing Verb Tenses

Remember, verb tenses in sentences are used to tell the reader what time an event takes place. In writing, one of the most common mistakes students make is to mixing present tense and past tense verbs. Mixing verb tenses can make your writing awkward and confusing to your reader.

The door opened, and my nephew comes into the kitchen and grinned.

In this sentence *opened* and *grinned* are past tense, and *comes* is present tense. The shift from past to present and back to past leaves your reader wondering about the time these actions take place. To make your writing clear and effective, choose a verb tense, or time, of your writing and stick to it.

Guided Practice:

Paragraph 1: Change these present tense verbs to past tense verbs in Paragraph 2.

   My uncle <u>is</u> a clown, and he <u>loves</u> his job. He and his fellow clowns <u>make</u> people happy. Audiences <u>laugh</u> in hearty anticipation of the clowns' next antics. People of all ages <u>forget</u> their troubles while they <u>are</u> <u>entertained</u> by these master entertainers. The clown act <u>is</u> truly astounding!

Paragraph 2: Past Tense

   My uncle _____ a clown, and he _____ his job. He and his fellow clowns _____ people happy. Audiences _____ in hearty anticipation of the clowns' next antics. People of all ages _____ their troubles while they _____ _____ by these master entertainers. The clown act _____ truly astounding!

Paragraph 3: Change these mixed verb tenses to past tense verbs in Paragraph 4 and present tense verbs in Paragraph 5.

   My brother <u>is</u> a champion swimmer. His strokes <u>were</u> smooth and perfect as he <u>slices</u> through the water with ease. Whenever he <u>swims</u>, my brother always <u>reminded</u> me of an otter; he <u>loves</u> to play in the water.

Paragraph 4: Past Tense

   My brother _____ a champion swimmer. His strokes _____ smooth and perfect as he _____ through the water with ease. Whenever he _____, my brother always _____ me of an otter; he _____ to play in the water.

Paragraph 5: Present Tense

   My brother _____ a champion swimmer. His strokes _____ smooth and perfect as he _____ through the water with ease. Whenever he _____, my brother always _____ me of an otter; he _____ to play in the water.

CHAPTER 25 LESSON 1 SKILL TEST A
(Student Page 226)

Paragraph 1: Change the past tense verbs to present tense verbs in Paragraph 2.

    I <u>looked</u> at Butch and <u>shook</u> my head. Butch <u>was</u> my guard dog. He <u>looked</u> ferocious, he <u>sounded</u> ferocious, and he <u>had</u> the pedigree for being a ferocious dog since he <u>was</u> a Doberman. But Butch <u>was</u> a wimp! He <u>was</u> afraid of the dark, and he <u>ran</u> and <u>hid</u> if someone <u>yelled</u> at him. Butch also <u>loved</u> strangers and <u>tagged</u> happily along after he <u>greeted</u> them. As I <u>continued</u> to shake my head, Butch <u>walked</u> over and <u>laid</u> his head in my lap. As he <u>looked</u> at me with those loving, trusting eyes, my heart <u>melted</u>. I <u>loved</u> my big wimp.

Paragraph 2: Present Tense

    I _____ at Butch and _____ my head. Butch _____ my guard dog. He _____ ferocious, he _____ ferocious, and he _____ the pedigree for being a ferocious dog since he _____ a Doberman. But Butch _____ a wimp! He _____ afraid of the dark, and he _____ and _____ if someone _____ at him. Butch also _____ strangers and _____ happily along after he _____ them. As I _____ to shake my head, Butch _____ over and _____ his head in my lap. As he _____ at me with those loving, trusting eyes, my heart _____. I _____ my big wimp.

Paragraph 3: Change the mixed verb tenses to past tense verbs in Paragraph 4 and present tense verbs in Paragraph 5.

    Cody <u>practices</u> his trumpet solo every afternoon after school. His sisters <u>complained</u> that the noise <u>interfered</u> with their television viewing. Cody <u>informs</u> his sisters that he <u>made</u> music, not noise. When Cody's dog <u>begins</u> howling, his sisters <u>giggled</u> and <u>run</u> from the room. Soon they <u>reappear</u> with three pairs of ear muffs, one pair for each of them and one pair for the dog.

Paragraph 4: Past Tense

    Cody _____ his trumpet solo every afternoon after school. His sisters _____ that the noise _____ with their television viewing. Cody _____ his sisters that he _____ music, not noise. When Cody's dog _____ howling, his sisters _____ and _____ from the room. Soon they _____ with three pairs of ear muffs, one pair for each of them and one pair for the dog.

Paragraph 5: Present Tense

    Cody _____ his trumpet solo every afternoon after school. His sisters _____ that the noise _____ with their television viewing. Cody _____ his sisters that he _____ music, not noise. When Cody's dog _____ howling, his sisters _____ and _____ from the room. Soon they _____ with three pairs of ear muffs, one pair for each of them and one pair for the dog.

CHAPTER 25 LESSON 2 SKILL TEST B
(Student Page 228)

Exercise 1: Underline the verb or verb phrase in each sentence. Then, identify the voice of the verb by writing **A** or **P** for Active or Passive in the blank.

_____ 1. The aardvark shuffled off in search of ants.

_____ 2. I trust you completely.

_____ 3. The trees along West Main have been cut down.

_____ 4. Did you drive the car?

_____ 5. The birdseed was left on the ground.

_____ 6. The leaf floated on the water.

_____ 7. Your name is being called.

_____ 8. All the bears will be fighting over that honey.

_____ 9. Ann and Donna were selected as cheerleaders.

_____ 10. The squirrel carried the pecans to his nest in the oak tree.

_____ 11. Mrs. Rickard was thinking of a tough assignment for Friday.

Directions: Write an active sentence and a passive sentence using the words **wolf** and **stalk**. You choose the tense of the verb.

12.

13.

Exercise 2: Underline each verb or verb phrase. In the first column, identify the verb tense by writing its corresponding number in the blank from the following list: (1) Present Tense (2) Past Tense (3) Future Tense (4) Present Perfect Tense (5) Past Perfect Tense (6) Future Perfect Tense (7) Progressive Form (8) Emphatic Form. Then, in the second column, write **R** or **I** for Regular or Irregular. (*Progressive and emphatic verbs are identified by form without noting the tense.*)

Verb Tense	R or I

14. The uneasy passenger did change his seat several times on the plane.

15. Both girls have mailed their letters.

16. All the tourists were waving from the deck of the ship.

17. Every day we sit at the same table in the cafeteria.

Exercise 3: Conjugate the verb *give* in the chart below.

Conjugation of the Verb Give					
Write the names of the four principal parts:					
Present	Past	Future	Present Perfect	Past Perfect	Future Perfect
(No helping verbs)	(No helping verbs)	(will or shall)	(has or have)	(had)	(will/shall) + have
Singular　Plural					

Simple Progressive Forms			Perfect Progressive Forms			Simple Emphatic	
am/is/are	was/were	will/shall + be	has/have + been	had + been	will/shall + have been	do/does	did

CHAPTER 25 LESSON 2 SKILL TEST C
(Student Page 229)

Paragraph 1: Change the present tense verbs to past tense verbs in Paragraph 2.

Not too far from where I <u>live</u>, a young couple <u>make</u> their home in a little brown house. They <u>do</u> not <u>have</u> any children. What they <u>do have are</u> two brightly colored macaws that they <u>bring</u> out into their front yard on nice days. It <u>is</u> always fun to walk past their house when the macaws <u>are</u> <u>sitting</u> on their perches on the porch of the brown house. As I <u>approach</u>, the birds <u>become</u> talkative, and they often <u>call</u> out hilarious remarks as I <u>walk</u> past.

Paragraph 2: Past Tense

Not too far from where I _____, a young couple _____ their home in a little brown house. They _____ not _____ any children. What they _____ _____ _____ two brightly colored macaws that they _____ out into their front yard on nice days. It _____ always fun to walk past their house when the macaws _____ _____ on their perches on the porch of the brown house. As I _____, the birds _____ talkative, and they often _____ out hilarious remarks as I _____ past.

Paragraph 3: Change the mixed verb tenses to past tense verbs in Paragraph 4 and present tense verbs in Paragraph 5.

My little sister Stephanie <u>has</u> a very unusual pastime. She <u>catches</u> bees. She <u>owned</u> what we <u>call</u> a "bug box." It <u>was</u> a little framed box with screen walls. A little door <u>opens</u> at one end. First, Stephanie <u>trapped</u> the bee in a glass jar. Then, she <u>places</u> the mouth of the jar over the open "bug box" door. Finally, she <u>shakes</u> the bee into the box and <u>slammed</u> the door.

Paragraph 4: Past Tense

My little sister Stephanie _____ a very unusual pastime. She _____ bees. She _____ what we _____ a "bug box." It _____ a little framed box with screen walls. A little door _____ at one end. First, Stephanie _____ the bee in a glass jar. Then, she _____ the mouth of the jar over the open "bug box" door. Finally, she _____ the bee into the box and _____ the door.

Paragraph 5: Present Tense

My little sister Stephanie _____ a very unusual pastime. She _____ bees. She _____ what we _____ a "bug box." It _____ a little framed box with screen walls. A little door _____ at one end. First, Stephanie _____ the bee in a glass jar. Then, she _____ the mouth of the jar over the open "bug box" door. Finally, she _____ the bee into the box and _____ the door.

Level 7 Skill and Application Test Workbook

CHAPTER 25 LESSON 3 SKILL TEST D
(Student Page 230)

Exercise 1: Underline the verb or verb phrase in each sentence. Then, identify the voice of the verb by writing **A** or **P** for Active or Passive in the blank.

_____ 1. Clear the deck!

_____ 2. A large storm was brewing over the lake.

_____ 3. The bridge to the castle was guarded by two alligators in armor.

_____ 4. We were almost shocked by the faulty electrical outlet.

_____ 5. Does your dog Hector have fleas?

_____ 6. All the hazelnuts had been picked by noon.

_____ 7. Could you send Mrs. Graham a card?

_____ 8. The artist painted a beautiful picture of Cagle's Mill.

_____ 9. By midnight, the refrigerator had already been raided.

_____ 10. The evidence was collected by Investigator Hubbard.

Exercise 2: Write an active sentence and a passive sentence using the words **pizza** and **cook**. You choose the tense of the verb.

11.

12.

Exercise 3: Underline each verb or verb phrase. In the first column, identify the verb tense by writing its corresponding number in the blank from the following list: (1) Present Tense (2) Past Tense (3) Future Tense (4) Present Perfect Tense (5) Past Perfect Tense (6) Future Perfect Tense (7) Progressive Form (8) Emphatic Form. Then, in the second column, write **R** or **I** for Regular or Irregular. (*Progressive and emphatic verbs are identified by form without noting the tense.*)

Verb Tense	R or I

13. The nurses will be needing more supplies for their clinic.

14. Our gymnastics instructor has taught us a new floor exercise every day.

15. These suit pants fit perfectly at the waist.

16. Our parents had planned carefully for our hiking trip into the canyon.

17. Yesterday my horse hurt his leg on a barbed-wire fence.

Exercise 4: Conjugate the verb *cheer* in the chart below.

Conjugation of the Verb Cheer						
Write the names of the four principal parts:						
Present		Past	Future	Present Perfect	Past Perfect	Future Perfect
(No helping verbs)		(No helping verbs)	(will or shall)	(has or have)	(had)	(will/shall) + have
Singular	Plural					

Simple Progressive Forms			Perfect Progressive Forms		Simple Emphatic	
am/is/are	was/were	will/shall + be	has/have + been	had + been	will/shall + have been	do/does	did

CHAPTER 25 LESSON 3 SKILL TEST E
(Student Page 231)

Paragraph 1: Change the past tense verbs to present tense verbs in Paragraph 2.

One night Marti, her brother Seth, and I <u>went</u> to Costa Rico's for dinner. Our waitress evidently <u>was</u> new on the job. We all <u>ordered</u> the Enchilada Special. When our order <u>came</u>, it <u>was</u> tamales and guacamole. We all <u>liked</u> tamales as well as guacamole, but we <u>hadn't</u> <u>ordered</u> it tonight. We also <u>ordered</u> punch to drink, but what <u>did</u> we <u>get</u>? Iced tea. The final blow <u>came</u> when Marti <u>told</u> the waitress we <u>had</u> not <u>ordered</u> all this. The waitress <u>said</u> to Marti, "I'm so sorry, sir." At that point, we all <u>gave</u> up.

Paragraph 2: Present Tense

One night Marti, her brother Seth, and I _____ to Costa Rico's for dinner. Our waitress evidently _____ new on the job. We all _____ the Enchilada Special. When our order _____, it _____ tamales and guacamole. We all _____ tamales as well as guacamole, but we _____ _____ it tonight. We also _____ punch to drink, but what _____ we _____? Iced tea. The final blow _____ when Marti _____ the waitress we _____ not _____ all this. The waitress _____ to Marti, "I'm so sorry, sir." At that point, we all _____ up.

Paragraph 3: Change the mixed verb tenses to past tense verbs in Paragraph 4 and present tense verbs in Paragraph 5.

At 10 A.M. on a muggy June morning, I <u>am</u> <u>jogging</u> along when I <u>noticed</u> a very dark cloud moving in from the southwest. I <u>stop</u> for a minute at my mailbox, and I <u>heard</u> an ominous growl of thunder. As I <u>headed</u> up the driveway, I <u>freeze</u> in my steps as a blinding flash of air-to-ground lightning <u>hit</u> a tree about one hundred and fifty feet to my right. I <u>shot</u> into my house, <u>sailed</u> to the basement, and <u>bury</u> my head in a pile of freshly-laundered clothes.

Paragraph 4: Past Tense

At 10 A.M. on a muggy June morning, I _____ _____ along when I _____ a very dark cloud moving in from the southwest. I _____ for a minute at my mailbox, and I _____ an ominous growl of thunder. As I _____ up the driveway, I _____ in my steps as a blinding flash of air-to-ground lightning _____ a tree about one hundred and fifty feet to my right. I _____ into my house, _____ to the basement, and _____ my head in a pile of freshly-laundered clothes.

Paragraph 5: Present Tense

At 10 A.M. on a muggy June morning, I _____ _____ along when I _____ a very dark cloud moving in from the southwest. I _____ for a minute at my mailbox, and I _____ an ominous growl of thunder. As I _____ up the driveway, I _____ in my steps as a blinding flash of air-to-ground lightning _____ a tree about one hundred and fifty feet to my right. I _____ into my house, _____ to the basement, and _____ my head in a pile of freshly-laundered clothes.

CHAPTER 25 LESSON 4 SKILL TEST F
(Student Page 234)

Exercise 1: Underline the verb or verb phrase in each sentence. Then, identify the voice of the verb by writing **A** or **P** for Active or Passive in the blank.

_____ 1. The house was wired by an experienced electrician.

_____ 2. Bill tripped over the bottle and fell into the basement.

_____ 3. The old lady body-slammed the mugger.

_____ 4. In the hurricane, the houses were removed from their foundations.

_____ 5. At the bookstore, Sir Robbley was surrounded by autograph-seekers.

_____ 6. With a grip of steel, Mrs. Briggs grabbed the thief and ejected him from her office.

_____ 7. On the lily pads, the four frogs croaked a symphony.

_____ 8. Mr. White approached the intercom with three pages of announcements.

_____ 9. Among the branches of the large magnolia tree, the blossoms were opening.

Exercise 2: Write an active sentence and a passive sentence using the words **man** and **drive**. You choose the tense of the verb.

10.

11.

Exercise 3: Underline each verb or verb phrase. In the first column, identify the verb tense by writing its corresponding number in the blank from the following list: (1) Present Tense (2) Past Tense (3) Future Tense (4) Present Perfect Tense (5) Past Perfect Tense (6) Future Perfect Tense (7) Progressive Form (8) Emphatic Form. Then, in the second column, write **R** or **I** for Regular or Irregular. (_Progressive and emphatic verbs are identified by form without noting the tense._)

Verb Tense	R or I		
		12.	The intermediate class will swim twice the length of the pool.
		13.	Planes from the nearby military base fly overhead regularly.
		14.	Jack does appreciate everyone's hard work on the project.
		15.	The attentive class had listened carefully to the flight instructor.
		16.	The earthquake victims have taken the supplies to their shelter.

Exercise 4: Conjugate the verb _grow_ in the chart below.

Conjugation of the Verb _Grow_					
Write the names of the four principal parts:					
Present	Past	Future	Present Perfect	Past Perfect	Future Perfect
(No helping verbs)	(No helping verbs)	(will or shall)	(has or have)	(had)	(will/shall) + have
Singular / Plural					

Simple Progressive Forms			Perfect Progressive Forms		Simple Emphatic	
am/is/are	was/were	will/shall + be	has/have + been	had + been	will/shall + have been	do/does	did

CHAPTER 25 LESSON 4 SKILL TEST G
(Student Page 235)

Paragraph 1: Change the present tense verbs to past tense verbs in Paragraph 2.

Mrs. Noddley from Pleasant Springs <u>loves</u> to ride a moped. She <u>has</u> one that she <u>uses</u> frequently. Everyone in the neighborhood <u>knows</u> Mrs. Noddley, and they <u>smile</u> when they <u>see</u> her. Mrs. Noddley <u>waves</u> at everyone as she <u>rides</u> along on her vehicle. She often <u>wears</u> cut-off overalls and a red T-shirt with a straw hat as she <u>cruises</u> along. Strangers who <u>visit</u> Pleasant Springs <u>are</u> often <u>surprised</u> to see an eighty-five-year-old woman riding a moped.

Paragraph 2: Past Tense

Mrs. Noddley from Pleasant Springs _____ to ride a moped. She _____ one that she _____ frequently. Everyone in the neighborhood _____ Mrs. Noddley, and they _____ when they _____ her. Mrs. Noddley _____ at everyone as she _____ along on her vehicle. She often _____ cut-off overalls and a red T-shirt with a straw hat as she _____ along. Strangers who _____ Pleasant Springs _____ often _____ to see an eighty-five-year-old woman riding a moped.

Paragraph 3: Change the mixed verb tenses to past tense verbs in Paragraph 4 and present tense verbs in Paragraph 5.

Jeff <u>stayed</u> home while his parents <u>are</u> <u>visiting</u> relatives for the evening. Since it <u>looked</u> like rain, he <u>went</u> outside and <u>parks</u> his bike under the patio cover. Then, he <u>rushed</u> back to the house before it <u>rains</u>. Jeff <u>moaned</u> as he <u>realized</u> the front door <u>was</u> <u>locked</u>. He <u>looks</u> at the rain, and he <u>looked</u> at the locked door. Then, he <u>grins</u>. He <u>knew</u> just what to do. He <u>crawls</u> through the "emergency" window.

Paragraph 4: Past Tense

Jeff _____ home while his parents _____ _____ relatives for the evening. Since it _____ like rain, he _____ outside and _____ his bike under the patio cover. Then, he _____ back to the house before it _____. Jeff _____ as he _____ the front door _____ _____. He _____ at the rain, and he _____ at the locked door. Then, he _____. He _____ just what to do. He _____ through the "emergency" window.

Paragraph 5: Present Tense

Jeff _____ home while his parents _____ _____ relatives for the evening. Since it _____ like rain, he _____ outside and _____ his bike under the patio cover. Then, he _____ back to the house before it _____. Jeff _____ as he _____ the front door _____ _____. He _____ at the rain, and he _____ at the locked door. Then, he _____. He _____ just what to do. He _____ through the "emergency" window.

CHAPTER 25 LESSON 5 SKILL TEST H
(Student Page 236)

Student Writing Assignment #34: Essay from the outline of the oral lecture on *Bonsai*.

Exercise 1: Underline the verb or verb phrase in each sentence. Then, identify the voice of the verb by writing **A** or **P** for Active or Passive in the blank.

_____ 1. A barn owl could be seen in the field behind our farmhouse.

_____ 2. The elderly gentleman carefully selected vegetables from the bins at the market.

_____ 3. The elderly gentleman was selected as the town's outstanding citizen.

_____ 4. The yellow daisies bloomed by the side of the old country road.

_____ 5. Mrs. Rogers was driven to the hospital by her husband.

_____ 6. Coffee brewed in the pot over the open campfire.

_____ 7. The sleeping child was carried upstairs to her bedroom after dark.

_____ 8. Each child's picture was taped to the wall outside the classroom.

_____ 9. Rachel was tripped by the extension cord.

Exercise 2: Write an active sentence and a passive sentence using the words **raccoon** and **frighten**. You choose the tense of the verb.

10.

11.

Exercise 3: Underline each verb or verb phrase. In the first column, identify the verb tense by writing its corresponding number in the blank from the following list: (1) Present Tense (2) Past Tense (3) Future Tense (4) Present Perfect Tense (5) Past Perfect Tense (6) Future Perfect Tense (7) Progressive Form (8) Emphatic Form. Then, in the second column, write **R** or **I** for Regular or Irregular. (*Progressive and emphatic verbs are identified by form without noting the tense.*)

Verb Tense	R or I

12. The ice in the glass on the table melted quickly.

13. The frightened child had awakened suddenly from nightmares.

14. This heavy anchor does sink quickly to the bottom of the ocean.

15. The storyteller is telling an interesting tale about an old farmer.

16. Our group will be standing near the entrance to the park.

Exercise 4: Conjugate the verb *cry* in the chart below.

Conjugation of the Verb *Cry*							
Write the names of the four principal parts:								
Present		Past	Future	Present Perfect	Past Perfect	Future Perfect	
(No helping verbs)		(No helping verbs)	(will or shall)	(has or have)	(had)	(will/shall) + have	
Singular	Plural					
Simple Progressive Forms			Perfect Progressive Forms		Simple Emphatic	
am/is/are	was/were	will/shall + be	has/have + been	had + been	will/shall + have been	do/does	did

Level 7 Skill and Application Test Workbook

CHAPTER 25 LESSON 5 SKILL TEST I
(Student Page 237)

Paragraph 1: Change the mixed tense verbs to past tense verbs in Paragraph 2.

Mindy <u>reads</u> Richard Adams' book *Watership Down* and <u>likes</u> it so much that she <u>bought</u> a hardcover edition. She <u>says</u> it <u>was</u> a story about a number of rabbits who <u>leave</u> their warren to seek safety. It <u>seems</u> that their warren <u>is</u> endangered. The rabbits <u>faced</u> many dangers as they <u>travel</u> to their new home. Mindy <u>urges</u> me to read the book because she <u>thinks</u> it <u>was</u> very good.

Paragraph 2: Past Tense

Mindy _____ Richard Adams' book *Watership Down* and _____ it so much that she _____ a hardcover edition. She _____ it _____ a story about a number of rabbits who _____ their warren to seek safety. It _____ that their warren _____ endangered. The rabbits _____ many dangers as they _____ to their new home. Mindy _____ me to read the book because she _____ it _____ very good.

Paragraph 3: Change the mixed verb tenses to present tense verbs in Paragraph 4.

I <u>had</u> <u>visited</u> three national parks this summer and <u>have</u> <u>studied</u> the different kinds of wildlife in each park. The first park <u>is</u> Yosemite National Park. In this park, it <u>was</u> very common for bears to raid campsites at night. Also, in the high country, a traveler <u>saw</u> elk or moose if he <u>is</u> lucky. The second national park <u>was</u> the Grand Canyon. On the rim of the Grand Canyon, squirrels, chipmunks, and canyon jays <u>beg</u> for food from tourists. Down in the canyon itself, rattlesnakes, cougars, and even coati mundis <u>roamed</u>. The third national park <u>was</u> the Everglades. Since this park <u>is</u> a great marsh, it <u>had</u> many types of waterfowl as well as fish. Probably its most popular animal with tourists <u>is</u> the alligator. Many different types of animals <u>lived</u> in the parks of the United States, and travelers <u>had</u> a chance to see many of them in such parks as Yosemite National Park in California, the Grand Canyon in Arizona, and the Everglades in Florida.

Paragraph 4: Present Tense

I _____ _____ three national parks this summer and _____ _____ the different kinds of wildlife in each park. The first park _____ Yosemite National Park. In this park, it _____ very common for bears to raid campsites at night. Also, in the high country, a traveler _____ elk or moose if he _____ lucky. The second national park _____ the Grand Canyon. On the rim of the Grand Canyon, squirrels, chipmunks, and canyon jays _____ for food from tourists. Down in the canyon itself, rattlesnakes, cougars, and even coati mundis _____. The third national park _____ the Everglades. Since this park _____ a great marsh, it _____ many types of waterfowl as well as fish. Probably its most popular animal with tourists _____ the alligator. Many different types of animals _____ in the parks of the United States, and travelers _____ a chance to see many of them in such parks as Yosemite National Park in California, the Grand Canyon in Arizona, and the Everglades in Florida.

CHAPTER 26 LESSON 1 SKILL TEST A
(Student Page 239)

Exercise 1: Put parentheses around the prepositional phrases in each sentence. Write **Adj** or **Adv** above each phrase to tell whether it is an adjective or adverb phrase. Then, write the word each phrase modifies beside the **Adj** or **Adv** label.

1. The best skiers in the group headed for the ski jump.
2. The illustrator in the museum drew with charcoal.
3. Above us the fireworks exploded brilliantly in the sky.
4. Jack London wrote many stories about Alaska.
5. We hid behind the tree.
6. Anna is the one in the pretty red suit.
7. My brother drove Dad's car down Main Street during the rush hour.
8. The lady with the funny purse walked along the street.
9. Bring me the book on the desk by the window.
10. The man in the gas station found a puppy under his hood.
11. All of us eyed the cake hungrily.
12. Everyone in the room laughed at the funny joke.
13. Our house is a cottage with white trim.
14. One of the longest rivers in America is the Columbia.
15. The club members are planning an overnight hike after school.

Exercise 2: Underline the verb or verb phrase in each sentence. Then, identify the voice of the verb by writing **A** or **P** for Active or Passive in the blank.

_____ 16. The smelly cans of garbage in the alley were collected every Tuesday morning.
_____ 17. Mr. Keys, the museum director, removed several exquisite art pieces from the display.
_____ 18. Mr. Keys was removed from the art museum on Friday.
_____ 19. My uncle's prized antique car was polished for the local antique car show.
_____ 20. My uncle polished his prized antique car for the local antique car show.

Exercise 3: Write an active sentence and a passive sentence using the words **parents** and **call**. You choose the tense of the verb.

21.

22.

CHAPTER 26 LESSON 1 SKILL TEST B
(Student Page 240)

Exercise 4: Underline each verb or verb phrase. In the first column, identify the verb tense by writing its corresponding number in the blank from the following list: (1) Present Tense (2) Past Tense (3) Future Tense (4) Present Perfect Tense (5) Past Perfect Tense (6) Future Perfect Tense (7) Progressive Form (8) Emphatic Form. Then, in the second column, write **R** or **I** for Regular or Irregular. (*Progressive and emphatic verbs are identified by form without noting the tense.*)

Verb Tense	R or I	
		23. The pageant contestant has already sung her song for the judges.
		24. The hunters had not looked for squirrels in those woods.
		25. These two boys do understand their math homework.
		26. My neighbor will have already heard about the new garbage collection days.
		27. Rhonda will read the whole book this weekend.

Exercise 5: Conjugate the verb *write* in the chart below.

Conjugation of the Verb *Write*					
Write the names of the four principal parts:					
Present	**Past**	**Future**	**Present Perfect**	**Past Perfect**	**Future Perfect**
(No helping verbs)	(No helping verbs)	(will or shall)	(has or have)	(had)	(will/shall) + have
Singular Plural					

Progressive form			Emphatic form	
present (am/is/are)	past (was/were)	future (will+be)	present (do/does)	past (did)

Paragraph 1: Change the present tense verbs to past tense verbs in Paragraph 2.

I <u>am</u> <u>sitting</u> in front of the fireplace, and the flames <u>are</u> <u>laughing</u> at me as they <u>lick</u> at the large oak log. I <u>am</u> <u>thinking</u> that I <u>need</u> a good movie to watch, but I <u>do</u> not <u>want</u> to travel to a video store. Also, the potato chips I <u>am</u> <u>munching</u> and the hot chocolate I <u>am</u> <u>drinking</u> <u>convince</u> me that I <u>do</u> not <u>want</u> to leave my comfortable spot on the couch. Suddenly I <u>spy</u> an old, dusty book in the corner of my shelf. As I <u>stare</u> at the book, I slowly <u>realize</u> that I <u>have</u> not <u>read</u> a book in years. My hands <u>tremble</u> in excitement as I <u>open</u> the book and <u>begin</u> to read.

Paragraph 2: Past Tense

I _____ _____ in front of the fireplace, and the flames _____ _____ at me as they _____ at the large oak log. I _____ _____ that I _____ a good movie to watch, but I _____ not _____ to travel to a video store. Also, the potato chips I _____ _____ and the hot chocolate I _____ _____ _____ me that I _____ not _____ to leave my comfortable spot on the couch. Suddenly I _____ an old, dusty book in the corner of my shelf. As I _____ at the book, I slowly _____ that I _____ not _____ a book in years. My hands _____ in excitement as I _____ the book and _____ to read.

CHAPTER 26 LESSON 2 SKILL TEST C
(Student Page 241)

Exercise 1: Put parentheses around the prepositional phrases in each sentence. Write **Adj** or **Adv** above each phrase to tell whether it is an adjective or adverb phrase. Then, write the word each phrase modifies beside the **Adj** or **Adv** label.

1. The boats on the water raced everywhere.
2. They will start early in the morning.
3. During library time I am reading a book about oceanography.
4. The adult snake curled around its eggs in its cage.
5. The mosquitoes in the park by the lake swarmed the unsuspecting campers.
6. The computer in Dad's office was extremely powerful.
7. The jazz band will play in the pavilion by the river.
8. The flowers from Gil were placed on the table in the study.
9. On the plane I usually read several magazines.
10. The colorful kite with the long tail fluttered gaily in the air above the houses and trees.
11. At the Mexican restaurant our family ate enchiladas and cheese dip for an hour.
12. My friend from school is coming to my house after dinner.
13. On Saturday my father took us to the ball game.
14. A few of the animals in the national park are found on the endangered species list.
15. Our neighbors across the street work in their yard in the evenings.

Exercise 2: Underline the verb or verb phrase in each sentence. Then, identify the voice of the verb by writing **A** or **P** for Active or Passive in the blank.

_____ 16. An expert tailor was consulted about the latest designs for our fashion show.

_____ 17. The coach of our football team was dunked in the dunking booth at our school carnival.

_____ 18. The cans of tuna were opened and distributed quickly to the hungry cats.

_____ 19. A crop duster sprayed chemicals on the field of soybeans.

_____ 20. The two small girls happily picked daffodils on Round Mountain.

Exercise 3: Write an active sentence and a passive sentence using the words **lion** and **hunt**. You choose the tense of the verb.

21.

22.

CHAPTER 26 LESSON 2 SKILL TEST D
(Student Page 242)

Exercise 4: Underline each verb or verb phrase. In the first column, identify the verb tense by writing its corresponding number in the blank from the following list: (1) Present Tense (2) Past Tense (3) Future Tense (4) Present Perfect Tense (5) Past Perfect Tense (6) Future Perfect Tense (7) Progressive Form (8) Emphatic Form. Then, in the second column, write **R** or **I** for Regular or Irregular. (*Progressive and emphatic verbs are identified by form without noting the tense.*)

Verb Tense	R or I

23. David will have sung his song on the radio by now.

24. Several men painted the gym last weekend.

25. My older brother had fixed the flat tire already.

26. Our new puppy always barks at the cat.

27. The customer representative has listened very carefully to your complaint.

Exercise 5: Conjugate the verb *carry* in the chart below

Conjugation of the Verb *Carry*

Write the names of the four principal parts:

Present		Past	Future	Present Perfect	Past Perfect	Future Perfect
(No helping verbs)		(No helping verbs)	(will or shall)	(has or have)	(had)	(will/shall) + have
Singular	Plural					

Paragraph 1: Change the present tense verbs to past tense verbs in Paragraph 2.

Larry's mom <u>stops</u> Larry in the hallway and <u>asks</u> him to describe a messy kitchen. Larry <u>scratches</u> his head as he <u>thinks</u> how to describe a messy kitchen to his mother. It <u>is</u> hard for him to imagine a messy kitchen because his mom <u>keeps</u> such a clean kitchen. He <u>eyes</u> his mom with suspicion as he <u>begins</u> to describe a messy kitchen. He <u>describes</u> a sink with lots of dirty dishes. Then, he <u>describes</u> messy countertops, messy floors, and a messy kitchen table in such vivid detail that he <u>talks</u> for a full ten minutes. As Larry <u>stops</u> and <u>gasps</u> for breath, he <u>gives</u> his mother a victory grin and <u>waits</u> for her approval of his messy kitchen description. (*Continued in Lesson 4.*)

Paragraph 2: Past Tense

Larry's mom _____ Larry in the hallway and _____ him to describe a messy kitchen. Larry _____ his head as he _____ how to describe a messy kitchen to his mother. It _____ hard for him to imagine a messy kitchen because his mom _____ such a clean kitchen. He _____ his mom with suspicion as he _____ to describe a messy kitchen. He _____ a sink with lots of dirty dishes. Then, he _____ messy countertops, messy floors, and a messy kitchen table in such vivid detail that he _____ for a full ten minutes. As Larry _____ and _____ for breath, he _____ his mother a victory grin and _____ for her approval of his messy kitchen description.

Level 7 Skill and Application Test Workbook

CHAPTER 26 LESSON 3 SKILL TEST E
(Student Page 243)

> **Oral Lecture Exercise:** Follow the guidelines from Chapter 25 as your teacher reads an oral lecture. Your oral lecture will be titled *Piranha*.

Exercise 1: Put parentheses around the prepositional phrases in each sentence. Write **Adj** or **Adv** above each phrase to tell whether it is an adjective or adverb phrase. Then, write the word each phrase modifies beside the **Adj** or **Adv** label.

1. The shelves in the kitchen need two coats of paint.
2. In the early morning the news carrier left the newspaper in our box.
3. Before the concert my uncle tuned his violin in the orchestra pit.
4. The hands on the clock moved silently toward the deadline.
5. Beyond the gate, we could hear hungry coyotes on the prowl.
6. During the day the doctors in the emergency room handled several crisis situations.
7. The diamond jewelry was locked in the case at night.
8. A special consultant from the company advised us in a meeting about our insurance.
9. By noon my sister will have finished her interview for museum director.
10. Everyone at the theater enjoyed the movie premier.
11. Keith drove the speed boat down the river to the next dock.
12. He ran up the hill and into the house.
13. After work I stopped at the donut shop.
14. Show us the painting of the old church in our town.
15. After supper, the small children in our house go to bed.

Exercise 2: Underline the verb or verb phrase in each sentence. Then, identify the voice of the verb by writing **A** or **P** for Active or Passive in the blank.

_____ 16. At the castle, a heavy wooden door was slammed in my face.

_____ 17. Five buckets of blueberries were considered a good haul for an hour's work.

_____ 18. The black and white skunk poked curiously around the trash in the city dump.

_____ 19. Billy's new hat was found under the wood pile behind his store.

_____ 20. Billy found his new hat under the wood pile behind his store.

Exercise 3: Write an active sentence and a passive sentence using the words **elephants** and **alarm**. You choose the tense of the verb.

21.

22.

Level 7 Skill and Application Test Workbook

CHAPTER 26 LESSON 4 SKILL TEST F
(Student Page 244)

Student Writing Assignment #35: Lecture essay on *Piranha*.

Exercise 4: Underline each verb or verb phrase. In the first column, identify the verb tense by writing its corresponding number in the blank from the following list: (1) Present Tense (2) Past Tense (3) Future Tense (4) Present Perfect Tense (5) Past Perfect Tense (6) Future Perfect Tense (7) Progressive Form (8) Emphatic Form. Then, in the second column, write **R** or **I** for Regular or Irregular. (*Progressive and emphatic verbs are identified by form without noting the tense.*)

Verb Tense	R or I

1. My sister will be beginning her computer training tomorrow.
2. My parents have gone to Mexico this week for a sales meeting.
3. I will have completed all my assignments before the date of the final exam.
4. You do arrive promptly every day at dinner time.
5. The entire class had read a total of 500 books for the contest.

Exercise 5: Conjugate the verb *take* in the chart below.

Conjugation of the Verb *Take*					
Write the names of the four principal parts:					
Present	**Past**	**Future**	**Present Perfect**	**Past Perfect**	**Future Perfect**
(No helping verbs)	(No helping verbs)	(will or shall)	(has or have)	(had)	(will/shall) + have
Singular Plural					

Paragraph 1: Change the past tense verbs to present tense verbs in Paragraph 2.

Larry's mother <u>looked</u> at him with a big smile on her face as she <u>commented</u> on his vivid imagination. She <u>patted</u> his back and <u>told</u> him how accurate his description <u>was</u> of a messy kitchen. Then, she <u>held</u> his hand as she <u>led</u> him to her kitchen. As she <u>opened</u> the door, she <u>told</u> Larry that she now <u>wanted</u> him to describe how he <u>was going</u> to clean up the mess from his bunking party last night.

Larry <u>stared</u> at the messiest kitchen he <u>had</u> ever <u>seen</u>. His mother totally <u>ignored</u> his desperation. She <u>waved</u> good-bye to him as she <u>left</u> him to his cleaning.

Paragraph 2: Present Tense

Larry's mother _____ at him with a big smile on her face as she _____ on his vivid imagination. She _____ his back and _____ him how accurate his description _____ of a messy kitchen. Then, she _____ his hand as she _____ him to her kitchen. As she _____ the door, she _____ Larry that she now _____ him to describe how he _____ _____ to clean up the mess from his bunking party last night.

Larry _____ at the messiest kitchen he _____ ever _____. His mother totally _____ his desperation. She _____ good-bye to him as she _____ him to his cleaning.

CHAPTER 26 LESSON 5 SKILL TEST G
(Student Page 245)

Exercise 1: Underline each verb or verb phrase. In the first column, identify the verb tense by writing its corresponding number in the blank from the following list: (1) Present Tense (2) Past Tense (3) Future Tense (4) Present Perfect Tense (5) Past Perfect Tense (6) Future Perfect Tense (7) Progressive Form (8) Emphatic Form. Then, in the second column, write **R** or **I** for Regular or Irregular. (*Progressive and emphatic verbs are identified by form without noting the tense.*)

Verb Tense	R or I

1. Mrs. Blue's class did not understand all the concepts on the semester test.
2. After today the athlete will have jogged one hundred miles for his training.
3. That lucky girl found several old coins in her collection.
4. The yellow sunflowers have stood in a tall row by the fence all summer.
5. The cows and calves will eat hay in the field across the road.

Paragraph 1: Change the past tense verbs to present tense verbs in Paragraph 2.

Samantha <u>felt</u> sorry for herself. She <u>didn't</u> <u>have</u> any friends, and she <u>wasn't</u> <u>doing</u> well in school. She <u>decided</u> she <u>was</u> a failure at an early age. As she <u>walked</u> around in the park with her head down, she <u>felt</u> a pair of eyes on her. As Samantha <u>raised</u> her head, she <u>looked</u> directly into a pair of alert, blue eyes. The blue eyes <u>belonged</u> to a boy about her age in a bright orange cap. He <u>walked</u> quickly to her side and <u>enlisted</u> her help to supervise a tag game for kids from the shelter down the street. Later, as Samantha <u>walked</u> home, her head <u>was</u> <u>held</u> high, and her eyes <u>were</u> bright with the prospect of helping the shelter kids again tomorrow. With a spring in her step, Samantha <u>decided</u> she <u>wasn't</u> a failure after all. She <u>liked</u> her new friends at the shelter who <u>volunteered</u> their time after school and on weekends. She even <u>decided</u> that she <u>had</u> to do better in school since she <u>wanted</u> to become a counselor.

Paragraph 2: Present Tense

Samantha _____ sorry for herself. She _____ _____ any friends, and she _____ _____ well in school. She _____ she _____ a failure at an early age. As she _____ around in the park with her head down, she _____ a pair of eyes on her. As Samantha _____ her head, she _____ directly into a pair of alert, blue eyes. The blue eyes _____ to a boy about her age in a bright orange cap. He _____ quickly to her side and _____ her help to supervise a tag game for kids from the shelter down the street. Later, as Samantha _____ home, her head _____ _____ high, and her eyes _____ bright with the prospect of helping the shelter kids again tomorrow. With a spring in her step, Samantha _____ she _____ a failure after all. She _____ her new friends at the shelter who _____ their time after school and on weekends. She even _____ that she _____ to do better in school since she _____ to become a counselor.

CHAPTER 27 LESSON 1 SKILL TEST A
(Student Page 247)

Exercise 1: Classify each sentence. Then, write the participle in the first blank and the word it modifies in the second blank.

1. The cleaning lady mopped the floor. _____ modifies _____
2. The talking birds entertained us. _____ modifies _____
3. A chosen group of students attended the concert. _____ modifies _____
4. Grandmother could hear the water dripping. _____ modifies _____
5. Aunt Sue found the ripped curtain! _____ modifies _____
6. Six sliced peaches filled the bowl. _____ modifies _____
7. We saw the blossoming cherry trees. _____ modifies _____
8. The disturbed ants crawled away hurriedly. _____ modifies _____
9. Our frozen hands could not open the door. _____ modifies _____
10. The raging fire burned forty acres. _____ modifies _____
11. Station KWOT is proud of its large listening audience. _____ modifies _____
12. We were assigned a written report. _____ modifies _____
13. The honking geese landed on the marsh. _____ modifies _____
14. Allison found her broken necklace. _____ modifies _____
15. Jason could see the icicles melting outside. _____ modifies _____

Exercise 2: Underline each participle once and each verb twice, and write **P** or **V** above each participle or verb.

16. The torn pages of the old book were fragile.
17. I smelled bread baking.
18. Those barking dogs were annoying my sister.
19. That home run resulted in a broken window!
20. The window was broken during the game.
21. Juanita could hear the cows mooing.
22. The cows were mooing.
23. The slithering snakes frightened my kids!
24. A lighted pathway helped us after dark.
25. Two snakes slithered at the bottom of a cage.
26. A relaxing vacation is in my future.
27. Jan and Joe relaxed on their vacation.
28. My teacher lost her reading glasses.
29. Our class was reading a poem by Longfellow.

CHAPTER 27 LESSON 1 SKILL TEST B
(Student Page 248)

Exercise 3: Put parentheses around each prepositional phrase, and write **Adj** or **Adv** above each phrase to tell whether it is an adjective or adverb phrase. Then, write the word each phrase modifies beside the **Adj** and **Adv** label.

1. I borrowed the book on the desk from Jonathan.
2. The bird's nest in the cedar tree was built by sparrows.
3. Hungry children from the city sat silently beside the busy road.
4. By this evening every thank-you letter to the presenters should be written.
5. Under the couch I found a pair of mittens and five pennies.

Exercise 4: Complete the chart below by writing these eight pronouns in the correct column: *another, others, whose, these, that, their, him,* and *he*.

Demonstrative Pronouns		Indefinite Pronouns		Interrogative Pronoun	Personal Pronouns		
Singular	Plural	Singular	Plural		Subjective	Possessive	Objective
6.	7.	8.	9.	10.	11.	12.	13.

Exercise 5: Underline the correct pronoun choice.

14. (We, Us) ladies enjoyed the visit to the gallery.
15. (Who, Whom) is your favorite fiction author?
16. The friendly dog gave Sam and (I, me) a shake.
17. This is (she, her).
18. The cake was given to (he and I, him and me).
19. Please visit (we, us) players after the game.
20. For (who, whom) is this music being played?
21. Paul and (me, I) were discussing tennis.
22. This is (her, she) day to do the laundry.
23. (He and I, Him and me) gave everyone cake.

Exercise 6: Underline each indefinite pronoun, and write **S** or **P** for singular or plural above it. Then, underline the correct verb.

24. Many of the exotic birds (is, are) available.
25. Few of the buildings (has, have) elevators.
26. Some (study, studies) in their rooms.
27. Everyone (park, parks) his car in this lot.
28. Most of the pencils (has, have) erasers.
29. Most of the candy (has, have) coconut in it.
30. None of the telephones (was, were) antiques.
31. Nothing (upset, upsets) Mother like fighting.
32. Both (send, sends) their regards.
33. All of my socks (has, have) holes in them.

Exercise 7: Draw one line under the subject, and write **S** or **P** for singular or plural. Then, underline the correct verb and the correct possessive pronoun to agree with the subject.

34. Each of the gentlemen (ride, rides) (his, their) horse to the stable.
35. Some of the turtles (lay, lays) (its, their) eggs in the water.
36. Some of the coffee (has, have) lost (its, their) flavor.
37. Few in the crowd (like, likes) to see (his, their) team lose.

CHAPTER 27 LESSON 2 SKILL TEST C
(Student Page 249)

Exercise 1: Classify each sentence. Then, write the participle in the first blank and the word it modifies in the second blank.

1. Matt pulled his laughing brother out of the mud. _____ modifies _____
2. Randy handed Anna the damaged vase. _____ modifies _____
3. The scolded puppy crept under the bed. _____ modifies _____
4. The swimming team won first place. _____ modifies _____
5. Leah located the missing key. _____ modifies _____
6. The fallen tree stretched across the road. _____ modifies _____
7. The chimney was covered with creeping ivy. _____ modifies _____
8. Shannon carried the sign to the painted bench. _____ modifies _____
9. The smiling candidate greeted his supporters victoriously. _____ modifies _____
10. The elected officials met with the committee. _____ modifies _____
11. Everyone heard the girls singing. _____ modifies _____
12. Soldiers arrived at the deserted village. _____ modifies _____
13. Whispering pine trees swayed in the wind. _____ modifies _____
14. The cracked vase was damaged during the earthquake. _____ modifies _____
15. The freezing temperature killed the plants. _____ modifies _____

Exercise 2: Underline each participle once and each verb twice, and write **P** or **V** above each participle or verb.

16. The snoring man kept his wife up all night.
17. The man snored all night.
18. Broken dishes lay everywhere on the floor.
19. Dishes were broken by the running children.
20. Bells chimed in the distance.
21. We could hear bells chiming in the distance.
22. Covered wagons carried pioneers westward.
23. Wagons were covered with canvas cloth.
24. A drizzling rain dampened our high spirits.
25. Rain drizzled all during the day of our picnic.
26. Daisy cleaned her sleeping puppies.
27. Daisy's puppies were sleeping in the barn.
28. Buzzing bees surrounded the beekeeper.
29. The bees were buzzing around their hive.
30. Those boys were laughing at their own jokes!
31. Those laughing boys were telling jokes.

CHAPTER 27 LESSON 2 SKILL TEST D
(Student Page 250)

Exercise 3: Put parentheses around each prepositional phrase, and write **Adj** or **Adv** above each phrase to tell whether it is an adjective or adverb phrase. Then, write the word each phrase modifies beside the **Adj** or **Adv** label.

1. During the night the wind whipped at the shutters of my windows.
2. Someone at the game will win a free ticket to the tournament.
3. Everyone in our class will have finished his test in time.
4. The small brown bat clung to the brick wall outside the building.
5. Behind the shed Dad painted a wooden chair for Mother's birthday.

Exercise 4: Complete the chart below by writing these eight pronouns in the correct column: *somebody, both, which, this, those, we, mine,* and *her*.

Demonstrative Pronouns		Indefinite Pronouns		Interrogative Pronoun	Personal Pronouns		
Singular	Plural	Singular	Plural		Subjective	Possessive	Objective
6.	7.	8.	9.	10.	11.	12.	13.

Exercise 5: Underline the correct pronoun choice.

14. The door was unlocked for Rick and (him, he).
15. Please help (her and me, she and I) to the car.
16. (Who, Whom) is the speaker at our meeting?
17. The doctor will give (we, us) sisters a call later.
18. To (who, whom) was this order given?
19. You and (I, me) will arrive at six o'clock.
20. (We, Us) citizens demand a recount of votes.
21. Those flowers were bought for (we, us) girls.
22. (He and I, Him and her) will wait in line.
23. Dan and (I, me) talked on the phone to Dad.

Exercise 6: Underline each indefinite pronoun, and write **S** or **P** for singular or plural above it. Then, underline the correct verb.

24. Nobody in the cave (has, have) his own light.
25. None of the pigs (like, likes) bread for food.
26. Both of the shoes (fit, fits) my swollen feet.
27. All of the meat (was, were) on the table.
28. Anything (is, are) capable of happening today.
29. Most of the eggs (is, are) in the basket.
30. Many (has, have) their reports published.
31. Some of the coins (is, are) not on the shelf.
32. Few (want, wants) brownies for dessert.
33. Any of the trucks (ride, rides) smoothly.

Exercise 7: Draw one line under the subject and write **S** or **P** for singular or plural. Then, underline the correct verb and the correct possessive pronoun to agree with the subject.

34. No one in the room (enjoy, enjoys) (his, their) meal.
35. Both of the children (write, writes) (her, their) assignments on graph paper.
36. Everybody (talk, talks) to (himself, themselves) during the morning break.
37. One of the alligators (eat, eats) fish every day for (his, their) meal.

CHAPTER 27 LESSON 3 SKILL TEST E
(Student Page 252)

Exercise 1: Classify each sentence. Then, label each gerund with a **G** in front of the noun job.

1. We heard the sound of whistling.
2. Winning makes him happy.
3. Mowing has been a worthwhile project.
4. You can forget fighting.
5. His favorite sport will be swimming.
6. Delaying will make the boss angry.
7. She uses a mop for cleaning.
8. Cleaning can be a difficult job.
9. Some people enjoy cleaning.
10. For gardening, you need an open, sunny area.
11. The younger children disliked waiting.
12. The man's occupation is painting.
13. We liked your singing and dancing.
14. Kelly used an extra long pole for vaulting.
15. Reading is Lindsay's favorite hobby.

Exercise 2: Underline each participle and gerund once and each verb twice. Write **P**, **G**, or **V** above each participle, gerund, or verb.

16. Modeling is a glamorous occupation.
17. Beth modeled winter coats at the mall.
18. The kids used modeling clay for their animals.
19. For traveling, we need several small bags.
20. We need several small traveling bags.
21. We will travel with several small bags.
22. Our teacher made writing a fun subject.
23. Two teachers helped with our writing class.
24. The teacher writes examples on the board.
25. I need typing paper for my class.
26. Sue is typing her letter on special paper.
27. Sue bought special paper for typing.
28. Jon was running in the hall of the school.
29. Jon was punished for running.
30. I could hear running water upstairs.
31. Yelling makes my elderly aunt nervous.
32. Yelling children were heard in the street.
33. That lady always yells at her children!

CHAPTER 27 LESSON 3 SKILL TEST F
(Student Page 253)

Exercise 3: Put parentheses around each prepositional phrase and write **Adj** or **Adv** above each phrase to tell whether it is an adjective or adverb phrase. Then, write the word each phrase modifies beside the **Adj** or **Adv** label.

1. The stone bowls from the museum were originally painted in bright colors.
2. The men in the army listened silently to their leader's instructions.
3. Nobody in our music class brought his (or her) band instrument to class.
4. A flock of bewildered geese flew north for the winter.
5. During the storm, lightning hit the barn with all the hay.

Exercise 4: Complete the chart below by writing these eight pronouns in the correct column: *hers, it, those, others, everything, this, who,* and *him*.

Demonstrative Pronouns		Indefinite Pronouns		Interrogative Pronoun	Personal Pronouns		
Singular	Plural	Singular	Plural		Subjective	Possessive	Objective
6.	7.	8.	9.	10.	11.	12.	13.

Exercise 5: Underline the correct pronoun choice.

14. (She, Her) and Dad went to the game.
15. The winners were Louise and (I, me).
16. (We, Us) students need a leader.
17. The wolf frightened Jerry and (I, me).
18. Sam saw Sara and (I, me) at the dance.
19. Todd invited only (we, us) boys to the game.
20. These books are for Dan and (I, me).
21. (She, Her) and I are going shopping.
22. This is (he, him).
23. You and (he, him) have been selected.

Exercise 6: Underline each indefinite pronoun, and write **S** or **P** for singular or plural above it. Underline the correct verb.

24. All of the water (was, were) spilled.
25. Most of the water (was, were) spilled.
26. Some of the water (was, were) spilled.
27. All of the students (was, were) present.
28. Most of the students (was, were) present.
29. Neither of the cars (is, are) red.
30. Everyone (has, have) a duty to vote.
31. Most (is, are) willing to try.
32. Everyone (expect, expects) an answer.
33. None of the horses (trot, trots) smoothly.

Exercise 7: For each numbered word, write the singular possessive form in the first blank and the plural possessive form in the second blank.

Word	Singular Possessive	Plural Possessive	Word	Singular Possessive	Plural Possessive
34. teacher			37. house		
35. baby			38. man		
36. woman			39. city		

CHAPTER 27 LESSON 4 SKILL TEST G
(Student Page 254)

Exercise 1: Classify each sentence. Then, label each participle with a **P** and each gerund with a **G** in front of its job in the sentence.

1. His favorite water sport is skiing.
2. After the craft fair, Dorothy's hobby will be tole painting.
3. The chopped onions made a delicious onion salad.
4. With his driving, we desperately needed nerves of steel.
5. The blowing curtains scared my little sister.
6. The stolen pie was found by my dad.
7. The man's occupation is painting.
8. The stranger found my broken camera.
9. At the contest the spectators loudly cheered the band's superb marching.
10. Swarming bees stung the hungry bears.
11. The senate voted on the renewed health plan.
12. Today we happily celebrated his wedding.
13. Printing can be a big headache.
14. The constant coughing made me miserable.

Exercise 2: Underline each participle and gerund once and each verb twice, and write **P**, **G**, or **V** above each one.

15. Dad planted the wheat.
16. Planting is Dad's job.
17. The planted wheat grows after a big rain.
18. Planting is done in the spring.
19. Blowing leaves tumbled across the yard.
20. The leaves were blowing across the yard.
21. The fallen leaves were a sign of autumn.
22. The leaves were removed by raking.
23. My uncle yelled loudly at the ball game.
24. The crowd supported the team by yelling.
25. The yelling crowd supported the team.
26. Yelling was encouraged by the cheerleaders.
27. The cheerleaders continued yelling.
28. Writing comes easily to some.
29. My writing assignment is due tomorrow.
30. I am writing my term paper.

CHAPTER 27 LESSON 4 SKILL TEST H
(Student Page 255)

Exercise 3: Write only the pattern number in the blank beside each sentence. Classify only the pattern core in each sentence. Use these pattern core examples to guide you: **P1-SN V, P2-SN V-t DO, P3-SN V-t IO DO, P4-SN LV PrN, P5-SN LV PA, P6-SN V-t DO OCN, P7-SN V-t DO OCA**

P **2** 1. The seals in the first ring are playing ball with their keeper.

P **1** 2. The angry fat man yelled loudly at the very noisy boys in his doughnut shop.

P **7** 3. Exercise can make a person energetic.

P **2** 4. During the blinding rainstorm, Artie mistakenly made a wrong turn.

P **6** 5. We considered him a hero.

P **3** 6. Yesterday Jay gave Leroy three new tires for his old Ford truck.

P **1** 7. Across the long, swinging bridge, Anne casually walked to her aunt's house above the river.

P **4** 8. Soon Louise will become the richest woman in the South.

P **3** 9. In the middle of the night he left George a secret message on the steps outside his house.

P **2** 10. The troops had a late breakfast and an early supper today.

P **7** 11. The children from the elementary schools painted the posts blue and white.

P **4** 12. Those chickens on Mrs. Brown's farm became potluck for the hungry people of the village.

P **5** 13. The athletes seemed nervous before the final meet.

P **1** 14. Helga crept down the stairs in a suit of red thermal underwear with a baseball bat in her hand.

P **3** 15. Donnie gave Ray a bundle of sticks for his new wood stove.

P **1** 16. The expert student mechanic crawled under the frame of the old abandoned school bus.

P **1** 17. Soon the lazy water buffalo at the edge of the water sluggishly walked away in search of food.

P **4** 18. The queen has become a basket case.

P **7** 19. After the storm the desert sun left the desert dry.

P **5** 20. The tail of an opossum is long and scaly.

P **1** 21. At the sound of the horn, the long tan lizard rapidly leaped to the side of the dusty road.

P **2** 22. In the dark basement Sam suddenly saw a gray rat with a curled tail.

P **1** 23. The long, green fuzzy worm with the strange purple horns on its head slowly crept along beneath the brilliantly green leaves of the luscious strawberry plants in the back rows of the country garden.

Exercise 4: For each numbered word, write the singular possessive form in the first blank and the plural possessive form in the second blank.

Word	Singular Possessive	Plural Possessive	Word	Singular Possessive	Plural Possessive
24. Smith			27. mouse		
25. berry			28. glass		
26. goose			29. ox		

CHAPTER 27 LESSON 5 SKILL TEST I
(Student Page 258)

Exercise 1: Write **I** above the infinitive in each sentence. Then, classify each sentence and label the function of each word in the sentence.

1. The horse to ride is Chester.
2. To vote, he stepped into the booth.
3. I want to win.
4. I know the place to park.
5. Maria bribed the judges to win.
6. To exercise is healthy.
7. To call, you must press the button.
8. The family's choice was to fly.
9. Houses to buy are plentiful.
10. We need to laugh.
11. The lady bowed her head to cry.
12. His objective is to win.

Exercise 2: Underline the infinitive or prepositional phrase in each sentence. Then, write **I** for Infinitive or **PP** for prepositional phrase above it.

13. His whole family came to our country.
14. They worked hard to survive.
15. All the students had to study.
16. To walk was his only desire.
17. We traveled to Europe.
18. My brother likes to ski.
19. He reported to headquarters.
20. He wanted to read.
21. My sister returned to college.
22. Our grandmother came to visit yesterday.
23. He likes to travel.
24. The player to watch is Jim.
25. Phil walked quickly to the store.
26. Sally and Linda had to apologize.
27. He gave his help to needy families.
28. Rhonda wanted to help.
29. We hurried to the garden.
30. The water rushed to our steps.

Exercise 3: Underline each participle, gerund, or infinitive once, and underline each verb twice. Write **P, G, I,** or **V** above each participle, gerund, infinitive, or verb.

31. To help is the only answer.
32. Our church is helping in the rescue effort.
33. David lent a helping hand to the homeless.
34. Helping made me feel good inside.
35. The music director asked everyone to listen.
36. Listen to the flutes during this next selection.
37. Listening was difficult for the small children.
38. It was music to our listening ears.

Exercise 4: Write three sentences using an infinitive as a noun, an adjective, and an adverb. Label each sentence.

CHAPTER 27 LESSON 5 SKILL TEST J
(Student Page 259)

Exercise 5: Write only the pattern number in the blank beside each sentence. Classify only the pattern core in each sentence. Use these pattern core examples to guide you: **P1-SN V,   P2-SN V-t DO,   P3-SN V-t IO DO, P4-SN LV PrN,   P5-SN LV PA,   P6-SN V-t DO OCN,   P7-SN V-t DO OCA**

P____ 1. The bird on the dogwood limb is a yellow flycatcher.

P____ 2. The registered voters in Pope County elected Mr. Hydro county judge.

P____ 3. Immediately the barber handed Clyde a mirror for a quick look at his chopped haircut.

P____ 4. William is very excited and happy at the idea of a visit from a real movie star.

P____ 5. The tall giant broke the limb over the head of the ugly monster.

P____ 6. Around the frantic settlers, the hostile Indians moved in a widening circle.

P____ 7. Mrs. Dustin delightfully named her new baby girl Angelica.

P____ 8. That pizza from the refrigerator tastes somewhat moldy.

P____ 9. Did Anthony walk quietly through the hall on the way to the Math Department?

P____ 10. Bring me the contributions and gifts to the shelter for the homeless.

P____ 11. In the winter the fur of an ermine becomes white.

P____ 12. The stage managers will be you and Terry.

P____ 13. The businessmen considered him a success.

P____ 14. The best cooks in cooking class are Beth and Lynn.

P____ 15. Do you believe the commander of the army competent?

P____ 16. The haughty girl gave Sylvia a scornful look.

P____ 17. After a thrilling finish the crowd enthusiastically applauded the actors.

P____ 18. The insensitive students labeled him careless after his unnerving accident.

P____ 19. The sign over the gas pumps swayed in the wind with a creaking noise.

P____ 20. The company in Washington sent Harry and Linda a crate of pens.

P____ 21. In a moment of temptation, the weasel at the chicken house was thinking about a delicate taste of some tender fowl.

P____ 22. Into the middle of the crowd, the three skinny little bullfighters walked with the attitude of men in charge.

Exercise 6: For each numbered word, write the singular possessive form in the first blank and the plural possessive form in the second blank.

Word	Singular Possessive	Plural Possessive	Word	Singular Possessive	Plural Possessive
23. Miller			26. fish		
24. company			27. deer		
25. butterfly			28. wife		

CHAPTER 28 LESSON 1 SKILL TEST A
(Student Page 260)

Exercise 1: Write **I** above the infinitive in each sentence. Then, classify each sentence and label the function of each word in the sentence.

1. To believe is to see.
2. This is the picture to take.
3. The librarian prefers to read.
4. Sherry loves to paint.
5. The teacher to have is Mrs. Dewitt.
6. The dog obviously wants to eat.
7. To boast is poor taste.
8. The rooster likes to crow.
9. To reduce, she went to a fitness center.
10. This is the team to beat.
11. They went to the beach to swim.
12. Our plan was to leave.
13. To cooperate produces good relationships.
14. You will have to work.
15. We wanted to sing.
16. Dave learned to sing.
17. They tried to run.
18. To swim is my favorite pastime.

Exercise 2: Underline the infinitive or prepositional phrase in each sentence. Then, write **I** for Infinitive or **PP** for prepositional phrase above it.

19. Mr. Smith came to the office.
20. We went to the park.
21. We wanted to swim.
22. We stayed to the end.
23. We tried to dive.
24. The boys are going to win.
25. The boys are going to the game.
26. My younger brother wanted to drive.
27. We all drove to the beach.
28. The students were told to study.
29. He ran to the house.
30. All the students plan to go.
31. The children want to leave.
32. He walked to the door.
33. He had always wanted to travel.
34. Dad sent roses to Mom.
35. Hand the mail to Chris.
36. To work is a necessity.

CHAPTER 28 LESSON 1 SKILL TEST B
(Student Page 261)

Exercise 3: Underline the verbals and identify each one with an abbreviation and function. Gerunds: *GSN, GDO, GOP, GPrN,* or *GOCN.* Participles: *PAdj.* Infinitives: *IAdj, IAdv, ISN, IDO,* or *IPrN.*

Infinitives

1. To act is Claudia's greatest ambition.

2. The house to buy is on the corner.

3. The little children at the park loved to play.

4. My neighbor's dog loves to bite.

Gerunds

5. Today we happily celebrated his arriving.

6. By studying he passed the test.

7. Dreaming is an interesting occupation.

8. The student enjoyed outlining.

Participles

9. We watched the rippling stream.

10. The talking birds entertained us.

11. The fire department rescued the stranded kitten.

12. This is her chosen occupation.

Exercise 4: Underline the verbals and identify each one with an abbreviation and function. Gerunds: *GSN, GDO, GOP, GPrN,* or *GOCN.* Participles: *PAdj.* Infinitives: *IAdj, IAdv, ISN, IDO,* or *IPrN.*

13. The children wanted to help.

14. The smashed car lay in the ditch.

15. Writing is my favorite pastime.

16. The breaking glass made a loud sound.

17. Swimming is Julie's favorite sport.

18. This is the song to sing.

19. That pipe needs draining.

20. Jody relaxed by reading.

21. The reading teacher is very good.

22. My family loves to ski.

23. The ringing bells were loud.

24. Tanning can cause skin problems.

25. The growling dog walked toward Andrew.

26. To knit is difficult for some people.

CHAPTER 28 LESSON 2 SKILL TEST C
(Student Page 262)

Exercise 1: Underline the verbals and identify each one with an abbreviation and function. Gerunds: **GSN, GDO, GOP, GPrN,** or **GOCN**. Participles: **PAdj**. Infinitives: **IAdj, IAdv, ISN, IDO,** or **IPrN**.

Infinitives

1. Ed chose to cooperate.

2. James is the person to help.

3. She only came to watch.

4. To perform had always been his dream.

Gerunds

5. Playing is a child's way of life.

6. At the contest the spectators cheered the band's marching.

7. A good mental exercise is writing.

8. My brother is always tired of studying.

Participles

9. The stolen jewelry could not be found.

10. A scrubbing brush was used for the filthy floor.

11. The cooked apples tasted delicious.

12. The little girl was charmed by the talking doll.

Exercise 2: Underline the verbals and identify each one with an abbreviation and function. Gerunds: **GSN, GDO, GOP, GPrN,** or **GOCN**. Participles: **PAdj**. Infinitives: **IAdj, IAdv, ISN, IDO,** or **IPrN**.

13. The difficulty of moving bothered us.

14. To compete takes practice.

15. The spinning wheel whirled around.

16. His hobby is cooking.

17. We saw the lady fanning.

18. The students in my class like to talk.

19. The watching dog sprang forward.

20. The committee chose to adjourn.

21. Complaining will only cause trouble.

22. We left after paying.

23. We must learn to wait.

24. He earns money by painting.

25. The broken dish lay in pieces.

26. Kathleen studies to learn.

CHAPTER 28 LESSON 2 SKILL TEST D
(Student Page 263)

Exercise 3: Underline the verbal in each sentence. Write **P** for Participle, **G** for Gerund, and **I** for Infinitive in the blank at the end of each sentence.

1. The man to call is Sam J. Jones. _____
2. Entire villages failed to survive. _____
3. The cows were kept in a holding pen. _____
4. Building is a carpenter's occupation. _____
5. They were called the losing team. _____
6. To farm was his life's goal. _____
7. Building blocks are good toys for toddlers. _____
8. The determined boy finished the race. _____
9. By squinting, I could see the sign. _____
10. We wanted to travel. _____
11. Harvested grain was stored in the warehouse. _____
12. We were told to listen. _____
13. The sleeping baby spent his day in a cradle. _____
14. The librarian promoted reading. _____
15. The men will enjoy golfing. _____
16. We heard the wind blowing. _____
17. To leave would be a mistake. _____
18. The excited scientist had discovered a cure. _____
19. My uncle always liked to whistle. _____
20. My uncle destroyed his health by smoking. _____
21. The frightened mother snatched her child and ran. _____
22. After our vacation, we needed to rest. _____
23. The x-ray showed a broken bone. _____
24. My laundry needs washing. _____

CHAPTER 28 LESSON 3 SKILL TEST E
(Student Page 266)

Exercise 1: Underline the verbal phrases and identify each one with an abbreviation and function. Gerunds: **GSN, GDO, GOP, GPrN,** or **GOCN**. Participles: **PAdj**. Infinitives: **IAdj, IAdv, ISN, IDO,** or **IPrN**.

Infinitive Phrases

1. Every effort to save the puppy succeeded.

2. Juan and Maria offered to help their father.

3. Our plan was to make a sand castle.

4. Everyone came to see the last game.

5. Mother was anxious to have a new house.

6. We came to encourage the Quiz Bowl candidates.

7. Our decision to buy a boat was a foolish one.

8. To meet the President was a great privilege.

Gerund Phrases

9. Hearing sleigh bells brought back memories.

10. I remember singing in the play.

11. Dan's job is running the company.

12. The time for asking questions is at the end of the meeting.

13. My brothers enjoy working with their hands.

14. My greatest goal was getting an education.

15. The younger children disliked waiting for their food.

16. Sipping hot cider through a straw was a fun idea on a cold day.

Participial Phrases

17. The football team wearing red jerseys stumbled off the field in defeat.

18. The man holding the large box walked through the curious crowd.

19. The teacher opening her door is the club advisor.

20. The girl getting in the car found her purse.

21. They spilled the water steaming in the pot.

CHAPTER 28 LESSON 3 SKILL TEST F
(Student Page 267)

Exercise 2: Underline the verbal phrase in each sentence. Write **P** for a Participial Phrase, **G** for a Gerund Phrase, and **I** for an Infinitive Phrase in the blank at the end of each sentence.

1. His assignment was to go to the store. _____

2. By winning at table tennis, he won $100. _____

3. The pies cooling in the window smelled good. _____

4. To leap off a cliff became the job of the stunt man. _____

5. The couple enjoyed walking in the park. _____

6. The time to call at my house is not midnight. _____

7. Campaigning for office is costly. _____

8. Rachel does not like painting in acrylics. _____

9. The tourist standing near the falls almost fell in. _____

10. We stood before the gate guarded by twenty men. _____

11. He flew to Chicago to visit with his cousin. _____

12. To write with ease, one must practice. _____

13. The athlete running at top speed won the marathon. _____

14. To hide the bone delighted Snoopy. _____

15. I couldn't remember learning that dance. _____

16. The tourists climbing up the ladder peered into the Indian ruin. _____

17. Working on the railroad provided a good income for our family. _____

18. He was told to listen for their return. _____

19. We watched Mr. Harris washing his car. _____

20. Jan always wants to win at card games. _____

21. My mother encouraged playing in the band. _____

22. We came to hear the music. _____

23. Thinking of everything is a requirement for this job! _____

CHAPTER 28 LESSON 4 SKILL TEST G
(Student Page 268)

Exercise 1: Underline the verbal phrases and identify each one with an abbreviation and function. Gerund Phrases: **GSN, GDO, GOP, GPrN,** or **GOCN**. Participial Phrases: **PAdj**. Infinitive Phrases: **IAdj, IAdv, ISN, IDO,** or **IPrN**.

Infinitive Phrases

1. That was an event to erase from your memory.

2. Alexis forgot to signal with the turnlight.

3. To sit by the fire is a pleasant experience.

4. The congressman's purpose was to win in the big election.

5. You only came to my house to visit with my uncle.

6. One of Aladdin's three wishes was to be a prince.

7. To be the winner is an honor.

Gerund Phrases

8. Awakening before daybreak can be a problem.

9. The mechanic just finished working on my car.

10. Standing in line for a ticket was necessary.

11. Great-grandmother remembers traveling in a hand-cranked car.

12. Janet's job was helping in the kitchen.

13. The children passed the time by watching the seals.

14. Walking at the mall became a daily routine.

Participial Phrases

15. Leaning with his ear to the keyhole, Eric tried to hear the conversation.

16. The duck swimming near the bank glided past our boat.

17. We saw the man shopping for a car.

18. The man answering our knock slammed the door in our faces.

19. The worker digging in the trench did not hear me.

CHAPTER 28 LESSON 4 SKILL TEST H
(Student Page 269)

Exercise 2: Underline the verbal phrase in each sentence. Write **P** for a Participial Phrase, **G** for a Gerund Phrase, and **I** for an Infinitive Phrase in the blank at the end of each sentence.

1. The lasagna cooked in the microwave was unusual. _____

2. By sneaking past the guard, the spy entered the castle. _____

3. The team trailing by ten points came from behind and won. _____

4. To sing like a nightingale is not easy for everyone. _____

5. The little boy remembered to wash behind his ears. _____

6. The director observed the whispering in the choir. _____

7. The author speaking at the podium talked about space travel. _____

8. Rebecca went to the museum to look at the paintings. _____

9. To pay by check is best. _____

10. To study with Seth is helpful. _____

11. We loved the cookies baked by Evelyn. _____

12. Aunt Sandy remembered to write a note. _____

13. They wanted to evacuate the building. _____

14. Sneezing on my paper was messing up my work. _____

15. The secretary wearing the blue suit is getting a raise. _____

16. All the children had a chance to vote in the election. _____

17. My brother hated shaving his beard. _____

18. The doctor wanted to operate on my toe. _____

19. Working with her roses made the elderly lady happy. _____

20. The elderly lady working with her roses was happy. _____

21. The committee asked to see the final reports. _____

22. Sailing to the Bahamas sounds like a great vacation. _____

23. To be an astronaut was his greatest ambition. _____

CHAPTER 28 LESSON 5 SKILL TEST I
(Student Page 270)

Exercise 1: Underline the verbal phrases and identify each one with an abbreviation and function. Gerund Phrases: **GSN, GDO, GOP, GPrN,** or **GOCN**. Participial Phrases: **PAdj**. Infinitive Phrases: **IAdj, IAdv, ISN, IDO,** or **IPrN**.

Infinitive Phrases

1. He preferred to watch from the stands.

2. To lead at the half encouraged them.

3. The game to play at the fire station is checkers.

4. The teenagers wanted to hurry to the concert.

5. A good exercise for one's heart is to walk at a fast pace.

6. To hide the Easter eggs for the children was a delightful activity.

7. We wanted to dance in the hotel's ballroom.

Gerund Phrases

8. To Lynn, swimming in the lake was scary.

9. Vaulting at the track meet was Priscilla's strongest event.

10. The girls' midnight recreation at the sleepover was fighting with pillows.

11. Becoming a member gave Gladys a sense of satisfaction.

12. I actually enjoy singing in the shower.

13. Tumbling down the hill is a new experience.

14. All campers must avoid stepping in poison ivy.

Participial Phrases

15. The twins swimming in the lake found a large mussel shell.

16. Lisa located the key missing from her purse.

17. The ivy creeping over the chimney housed several birds' nests.

18. The chef carrying the wedding cake fell down the steps.

19. The students clapping in the stands shouted for their team.

20. She waited for the next flight going to Finland.

21. The donkey carried the supplies ordered by the doctor.

CHAPTER 28 LESSON 5 SKILL TEST J
(Student Page 271)

Exercise 2: Underline the verbal phrase in each sentence. Write *P* for a Participial Phrase, *G* for a Gerund Phrase, and *I* for an Infinitive Phrase in the blank at the end of each sentence.

1. Jeff decided to go to New York. _____

2. The horse tied to the fence belonged to Uncle Jack. _____

3. The cake bought at the store was fresh. _____

4. During our vacation, we discovered snorkeling on the reefs. _____

5. My older sister wanted to plan for her wedding. _____

6. The merchandise stolen from the store was recovered by the police. _____

7. I had to deliver the pizza. _____

8. Overeating during meals caused my weight gain. _____

9. We need to change the flat tire. _____

10. Dancing in the school play was embarrassing for me. _____

11. My new hobby is spelunking in northern Arkansas. _____

12. Everyone at the party liked the bread baked by Aunt Jewell. _____

13. Cutting with scissors is always a challenge for small children. _____

14. Typing on the computer was Mom's least favorite job at work. _____

15. The cookies eaten before lunch gave everyone a stomachache. _____

16. To dine at Ritzi's was a special birthday treat. _____

17. For the soldiers, to surrender to the enemy was unthinkable. _____

18. The trees downed by the storm were piled by the side of the road. _____

19. Last Saturday our group's job was raking leaves. _____

20. The money earned by Sally was spent for her family's food. _____

21. Our family bought a new tent for camping in the park. _____

22. Sandra enjoyed driving across the state. _____

23. The political candidate was congratulated for winning the election. _____

24. The present arriving from Ireland was for me. _____

CHAPTER 29 LESSON 1 SKILL TEST A
(Student Page 275)

Exercise 1: Number each **S-V** combination and write the number of clauses for each sentence in the blank.

_____ 1. Angelica owned a parakeet named Vigorous and kept him in a large, roomy cage.

_____ 2. Apparently Vigorous did not think that his cage was "roomy" enough.

_____ 3. One day when Angelica shut the cage door, she did not snap it.

_____ 4. Vigorous found that he could get out.

_____ 5. As Angelica entered the room, a flurry of feathers sailed toward her.

_____ 6. Vigorous perched on her head, and his owner was quite surprised.

_____ 7. Because my brother Carl's band instrument is drums, our home has become noisy.

_____ 8. Yesterday, as he came in the front door, he only mentioned drums, and I got a headache.

_____ 9. My dreams are turning into nightmares that are filled with giant drums.

_____ 10. Before the nightmare is over, the drums sprout legs and chase me through a gigantic percussion section.

_____ 11. I have told my brother that he must make his room soundproof.

_____ 12. The person who invented the drum is in trouble with me.

_____ 13. When Brian left his cap in the fork of the apple tree, it was "no big thing."

_____ 14. Three days later, he returned and found a robin with a half-built nest in his cap.

_____ 15. Since he had two other caps, he left it there.

_____ 16. As time passed, Brian watched his cap, and soon four eggs lay in the nest.

_____ 17. Before long, he saw four tiny brown heads over the edge of the nest because the four eggs had hatched.

CHAPTER 29 LESSON 2 SKILL TEST B
(Student Page 278)

Exercise 1: Number each **S-V** combination and write the number of clauses for each sentence in the blank. Put parentheses around any subordinate conjunctions and underline the independent clauses once and the dependent clauses twice.

_____ 1. We do not know how the bumblebee got into the van.

_____ 2. It could have happened while we were at the curio shop with the lawn decorations.

_____ 3. Fred cannot remember whether the bee had been with us before the stop.

_____ 4. Before we had driven one-half mile, Molly screamed.

_____ 5. As Derrick and James started swatting, the bee shot to the front of the vehicle.

_____ 6. Sarah hit at the little pest, and Fred swerved.

_____ 7. He slammed on the brakes, and the car behind our van rear-ended us.

_____ 8. As another car avoided the accident, it ran a semi-rig off the road and into a ditch.

_____ 9. We were thankful that no one was hurt.

_____ 10. Unfortunately, the bee escaped before we could give him his punishment.

_____ 11. Travis baked three dozen sugar cookies, but he ate twenty-four of them after lunch.

_____ 12. After the members discussed plans for the next meeting, they drew for a door prize.

_____ 13. Fortunately, Dewayne bought his plane ticket before the ticket prices went up.

_____ 14. Because I enjoy hiking, Dan and I walked the two miles into town.

_____ 15. Since I have so little time, I will write you a longer letter later.

_____ 16. We visited the Berkley Pit and learned facts about copper mining after we ate lunch.

_____ 17. While we were there, we learned the history of the stately buildings.

_____ 18. You may fish here provided you have a fishing license.

Level 7 Skill and Application Test Workbook

CHAPTER 29 LESSON 3 SKILL TEST C
(Student Page 281)

Exercise 1: Number each **S-V** combination and write the number of clauses for each sentence in the blank. Put parentheses around any **H, TH,** or **WH** words that introduce a dependent clause. Underline the independent clauses once and the dependent clauses twice.

_____ 1. You can always find ants wherever people are having picnics.

_____ 2. They are little creatures whose "noses" can sniff out food from miles away.

_____ 3. It does not matter where you securely set your food.

_____ 4. I have heard of few people who know of a plan to avoid ants.

_____ 5. A friend, whom I will not name, assured me of a foolproof method.

_____ 6. His idea, which was simple, was spraying the legs of the picnic table with insect repellant.

_____ 7. I do not know why I bothered with his suggestion.

_____ 8. Something that no one expects always happens.

_____ 9. The table whose legs I sprayed had an ant's nest under the tabletop.

_____ 10. Whatever I do, ants will join my picnic.

_____ 11. The boys ate whatever was in the refrigerator.

_____ 12. Mr. Murphy understood who the leader was.

_____ 13. The milk which you bought is spoiled.

_____ 14. We own the house where you once lived.

_____ 15. The girl whom he invited is Cassandra.

_____ 16. Did you tell Marcus that we are coming?

CHAPTER 29 LESSON 4 SKILL TEST D
(Student Page 283)

Exercise 1: Number each **S-V** combination and write the number of clauses for each sentence in the blank. Put parentheses around any introducers of dependent clauses. Underline the independent clauses once and the dependent clauses twice.

_____ 1. In the 1960's, my grandfather owned about two dozen chickens, which he kept in a "hen house."

_____ 2. While these fowls were not very impressive to others, to my grandparents they were eggs and fried chicken.

_____ 3. One night some creature invaded the hen house, and a great disorder broke out about 11 p.m.

_____ 4. My grandfather, thinking that a weasel had come for his eggs and fried chicken, grabbed his shotgun and hurried to the hen house.

_____ 5. Although he took his flashlight with him, the chickens were so frantic that he only saw a shadow across the floor.

_____ 6. Before the invader could escape, Granddaddy fired a shot.

_____ 7. The invader that he shot was not a weasel, but a skunk!

_____ 8. If he had hurried to the hen house before, he now "flew" in the opposite direction.

_____ 9. My grandmother took one sniff and knew what had happened.

_____ 10. After Granddaddy had burned his clothes and had taken three hot, soapy baths, the smell of the skunk was only faint.

_____ 11. Since my little sister and her friends had been in the pool all afternoon, they were starved!

_____ 12. That pickle and mustard sandwich that you made is great!

_____ 13. If the snow stops, we can build a six-foot snowman.

CHAPTER 29 LESSON 4 SKILL TEST E
(Student Page 284)

Exercise 1: Number each **S-V** combination and write the number of clauses for each sentence in the blank. Put parentheses around any introducers of dependent clauses. Underline the independent clauses once and the dependent clauses twice.

_____ 1. When Dan came home from school, he announced that he and his friends were going swimming at Bayou Bluff.

_____ 2. Bayou Bluff, which was a swimmer's paradise, offered all sorts of fun in the water.

_____ 3. It was a broad stream that flowed over huge boulders past towering bluffs.

_____ 4. A series of rapids eventually widened out into slow, deep water where diving and swimming were popular.

_____ 5. Dan and his buddies carried several inner tubes on which they would float the rapids.

_____ 6. Because the sun was so hot, Dan wore his new expensive sunglasses.

_____ 7. When he made his first trip down the rapids, he forgot that he was wearing his favorite "shades."

_____ 8. As he reached the second set of rapids, Dan was laughing and did not see a large extended rock.

_____ 9. Before he could change course, the tube hit the rock and flipped, and Dan was dumped.

_____ 10. His glasses flew off, and, although he and his friends dived for them for an hour, he never saw them again.

_____ 11. The dog will not attack you if you keep calm.

_____ 12. Chandra, whom the faculty selected, will represent the school at the convention.

_____ 13. Delia hid the candy whenever she left her room.

_____ 14. As the children watched, they saw where Mitchell put the box.

CHAPTER 29 LESSON 5 SKILL TEST F
(Student Page 287)

Exercise 1: Number each **S-V** combination and write the number of clauses for each sentence in the blank. Put parentheses around any introducers of dependent clauses. Underline the independent clauses once and the dependent clauses twice. Identify the type of dependent clause by writing **Adj** and the word it modifies in the two blanks at the end of the sentence.

_____ 1. The frosting which was all over his face was chocolate.   _____ _____

_____ 2. The man whose tie was green polka-dotted performed a series of magic tricks. _____ _____

_____ 3. The stewardess whom you stopped is my cousin.   _____ _____

_____ 4. He hired the two young men who worked hardest.   _____ _____

_____ 5. He had been imprisoned in a dungeon where no light could enter.   _____ _____

_____ 6. At the hour when most people were asleep, he left the house.   _____ _____

_____ 7. I could not explain the mess in which we found in the room.   _____ _____

_____ 8. The first runner who reaches the oak tree wins.   _____ _____

_____ 9. There goes the man who owns the jeep.   _____ _____

_____ 10. Beside the candle which was burning we found an old map.   _____ _____

_____ 11. The umbrella that we noticed belongs to Jill.   _____ _____

_____ 12. This is a time when you must listen.   _____ _____

_____ 13. I know the girl whom you chose.   _____ _____

On your notebook paper:

14. Write a sentence containing an adjective clause.

CHAPTER 30 LESSON 1 SKILL TEST A
(Student Page 289)

Exercise 1: Number each **S-V** combination and write the number of clauses for each sentence in the blank. Put parentheses around the subordinating conjunction that introduces a dependent clause used as an adverb. Underline each independent clause once and each dependent clause twice. Identify the type of dependent clause by writing **Adv** and the verb it modifies in the two blanks at the end of the sentence.

_____ 1. We will be with the team until we finish our practice. _____ _____

_____ 2. The little man lived where the stream flows blue. _____ _____

_____ 3. Our picnic will be perfect provided it does not rain. _____ _____

_____ 4. I have been working on my serve since you saw my last tennis game. _____ _____

_____ 5. Before the whistle blew, he had scored two more points. _____ _____

_____ 6. As he left the plane, he took the strange attaché case with him. _____ _____

_____ 7. When a bluebird flew in the window, Janelle was surprised. _____ _____

_____ 8. The postman enjoyed a cup of hot tea because it was a cold day. _____ _____

_____ 9. I hit a tree because my bike had no brakes. _____ _____

_____ 10. While I pop the popcorn, you bring in more wood. _____ _____

_____ 11. Since I have a new chessboard, we must have a game. _____ _____

_____ 12. The crowd yelled loudly as the cheerleaders came onto the court. _____ _____

_____ 13. Although I enjoy fruit yogurt, I love cappuccino better. _____ _____

_____ 14. When you are crossing the lawn, walk around the flowerbed. _____ _____

_____ 15. He will lend you his binoculars, provided you return them. _____ _____

On your notebook paper:

16. Write a sentence with an adverb clause in it. Tell what adverb question it answers.

CHAPTER 30 LESSON 2 SKILL TEST B
(Student Page 290)

Exercise 1: Number each **S-V** combination and write the number of clauses for each sentence in the blank. Put parentheses around any introducers of dependent clauses. Underline each independent clause once and each dependent clause twice. Identify the type of dependent clause by writing **Adj** or **Adv** and the word it modifies in the two blanks at the end of the sentence.

_____ 1. The girl who is on the balance beam is Anna.   _____ _____

_____ 2. After she has finished her performance, we will be leaving.   _____ _____

_____ 3. We congratulated the team that won.   _____ _____

_____ 4. I saw an old friend of mine as we walked across the parking lot.   _____ _____

_____ 5. This is the school where I once attended.   _____ _____

_____ 6. Mr. Franklin was a teacher whose class I loved.   _____ _____

_____ 7. I enjoyed the gymnastic meet since my friend won several awards.   _____ _____

_____ 8. Before my little sister could swim, she had a terrible fear of water.   _____ _____

_____ 9. She was even afraid of her wading pool, which was only six inches deep.   _____ _____

_____ 10. The time that she dreaded most was her evening bath.   _____ _____

_____ 11. When she cried loudly, I gave up!   _____ _____

_____ 12. I took her down to the pool for lessons because I could not teach swimming.   _____ _____

_____ 13. Now she has turned into a kid who is a regular "fish."   _____ _____

_____ 14. If she stays in water any more, her skin will go into a permanent shrivel.   _____ _____

On your notebook paper:

15. Write a sentence with adverb clause in it. Label it correctly.

16. Write a sentence with adjective clause in it. Label it correctly.

CHAPTER 30 LESSON 3 SKILL TEST C
(Student Page 293)

Exercise 1: Number each **S-V** combination and write the number of clauses for each sentence in the blank. Put parentheses around the introducer of the dependent clause used as a noun. Underline each independent clause once and each dependent clause twice.. Exception: When the noun clause is the **SN**, do not underline any clause in the sentence. Instead, put the noun clause used as a **SN** in Brackets. Also, notice that each noun clause's function has been Identified for you at the end of each sentence.

_____ 1. I believe that it is raining. __DO__

_____ 2. Joyce recognized whom you drew. __DO__

_____ 3. Chris sent the letter to whoever wanted it. __OP__

_____ 4. The principal knew why the student was dishonest. __DO__

_____ 5. He could not see where he was driving. __DO__

_____ 6. I can tutor whomever you send. __DO__

_____ 7. I remember whose mother bakes fantastic cookies. __DO__

_____ 8. He handed out invitations to whoever was there. __OP__

For Bonus Points: Using the Noun Clause as a Subject

_____ Bonus 1. That the radio is loud is obvious. __SN__

_____ Bonus 2. What he is doing helps. __SN__

CHAPTER 30 LESSON 4 SKILL TEST D
(Student Page 294)

Number each **S-V** combination and write the number of clauses for each sentence in the blank. Put parentheses around the introducer of each dependent clause. Underline each independent clause once and each dependent clause twice. **Exception:** When the noun clause is the **SN**, do not underline any clause in the sentence. Instead, put the noun clause used as a **SN** in Brackets. Also write the name of each dependent clause (**Adj, Adv,** or **N**) at the end of each sentence. Use the following guides to help you. **Guided Practice: Adv: 2 Adj: 1 N: 2 Exercise 1: Adv: 4 Adj: 2 N: 4**

Guided Practice:

___ 1. When the flea slipped, he fell off the dog's ear. _____

___ 2. I know whose car will win the race. _____

___ 3. The cliff diver never told us that he was afraid of heights. _____

___ 4. The snail that defeated the inchworm amazed everyone. _____

___ 5. Before you go to lunch, give Beth the report. _____

Exercise 1:

_____ 1. He gets mega-omelets because his father owns an ostrich farm. _____

_____ 2. Ricky sold the saddle to whoever offered him the most money. _____

_____ 3. The music that they love is classical. _____

_____ 4. She was a scuba diver who taught scuba lessons. _____

_____ 5. Since the inventor blew up his workshop, he was moved to the barn. _____

_____ 6. Rebecca told us how she found her way out of the jungle. _____

_____ 7. Lee, who was babysitting, found her three charges on the roof. _____

_____ 8. He told the story as I had hoped. _____

_____ 9. When the fish tugged on his line, Howard yanked. _____

For Bonus Points: Using the Noun Clause as a Subject

_____ 10. How you balance on that tightrope seems unbelievable. _____

CHAPTER 31 LESSON 1 SKILL TEST A
(Student Page 298)

Exercise 1: Underline the correct adjective or adverb choice in each sentence below. Write **Adj** or **Adv** and the word it modifies in the blanks at the end.

1. Our junior high wrestling team did (good, well) at the regional meet. _____ _____
2. Are you (sure, surely) about the correct departure time? _____ _____
3. A (real, really) inventor displayed his gadgets in a booth at the fair. _____ _____
4. Two of the pizzas tasted (real, really) delicious! _____ _____
5. Our pets were (sure, surely) the most unusual at the pet show. _____ _____
6. The student carpenters did a (good, well) job of framing the new house. _____ _____
7. The skiers will (sure, surely) stop for a rest at noon. _____ _____
8. Our teacher did not feel (good, well) after lunch. _____ _____
9. The results of the tests were (bad, badly). _____ _____
10. The girls sang their part of the song (bad, badly). _____ _____

Exercise 2: Underline the correct word choice in each sentence below. In the blank, write **N** for noun, **Adj** for adjective, and **V** for verb to tell how the word is used in the sentence.

11. The junior high (principal, principle) spoke with several students about their schedules. _____
12. The (affects, effects) of the earthquake have left the population in need of shelter and food. _____
13. The small children were most (affected, effected) by the frightening storm. _____
14. One scientific (principal, principle) that was emphasized was the law of gravity. _____
15. The (principal, principle) member of the committee visited our classroom to ask for our opinion. _____
16. The new governor has (affected, effected) better policies within the highway department. _____

Exercise 3: Underline the correct verb choice in each sentence below. In the blank, write **DO** if the verb has a direct object and **No DO** if it doesn't.

17. James is (sitting, setting) in the swing on the porch. _____
18. My uncle is (laying, lying) carpet on weekends for an extra job. _____
19. The dough for the homemade bread has (raised, risen) in the pan. _____
20. The artists have (set, sat) their supplies on the tables in the classroom. _____
21. Several dogs (lay, laid) in the doorway to the barn. _____
22. Three sleepy children (raised, rose) early before breakfast. _____
23. Grandpa has (raised, risen) the shelf for Grandma. _____
24. The beached whale had (laid, lain) on the shore for several days. _____
25. We are (setting, sitting) in our seats at the top of the stadium. _____

Exercise 4: Underline the correct verb choice in each sentence below.

26. We (was, were) helping my cousin feed his cows hay from the barn.
27. He (did, done) his chores every afternoon after school.
28. You (was, were) not on the list to get a refund.
29. I have (come, came) to pick up my father's paycheck.
30. Those youngsters had (gone, went) to the movies twice last week.

CHAPTER 31 LESSON 2 SKILL TEST B
(Student Page 300)

Exercise 1: Underline the correct adjective or adverb choice in each sentence below. Write **Adj** or **Adv** and the word it modifies in the blanks at the end.

1. The kindergartners listened (good, well) during story time. _____ _____
2. My aunt felt (bad, badly) about running out of cake at the wedding. _____ _____
3. Several of the young authors wrote (good, well) stories for our collection. _____ _____
4. We did (bad, badly) on Mrs. Green's science test last week. _____ _____ _____
5. Our mother looks (good, well) in her new hairstyle. _____ _____
6. I am (sure, surely) you will do a great job on your project. _____ _____
7. Those dogs have (sure, surely) eaten all their dog food by now. _____ _____
8. Most of the stolen jewelry contained (real, really) gems. _____ _____
9. I couldn't wait for some (real, really) spicy hot sauce from Taco Tom's. _____ _____
10. My baby brother had a (bad, badly) earache last night. _____ _____

Exercise 2: Underline the correct word choice in each sentence below. In the blank, write **N** for noun, **Adj** for adjective, and **V** for verb to tell how the word is used in the sentence.

11. A (principal, principle) part of the proposal includes a raise in taxes. _____
12. One (affect, effect) of the parent conference was improved study habits. _____
13. The voters were (affected, effected) by the candidate's speech. _____
14. The (principal, principle) of the new school has made a decision about new computer equipment. _____
15. The (principals, principles) of business law were discussed during the education conference. _____
16. Our present chairman (affected, effected) stricter rules for our committee. _____

Exercise 3: Underline the correct verb choice in each sentence below. In the blank, write **DO** if the verb has a direct object and **No DO** if it does not have a direct object.

17. Right now, several sacks of fertilizer (lay, lie) on the dock to be loaded. _____
18. Volunteers from the audience (raise, rise) their hands to play the games. _____
19. New sprouts are (raising, rising) from the ground in the garden. _____
20. Grandma's new chickens (lay, laid) colored eggs! _____
21. Please (set, sit) your painting equipment in the carport. _____
22. Our old parrot (sat, set) on his perch talking to our visitors. _____
23. Jason's wet clothes are (lying, laying) on the floor in the bathroom! _____
24. My little sister (lays, lies) her head on my pillow every night. _____
25. Two hundred soldiers (lay, laid) in the grave after the ground battle. _____

Exercise 4: Underline the correct verb choice in each sentence below.

26. The assembly workers have (did, done) a good job of meeting their quotas this month.
27. Charles has (came, come) to visit us every day this week.
28. You (was, were) able to hear the weather report on the radio.
29. I already (did, done) my report in the library.
30. Everyone has (gone, went) to the lake this weekend except me!

CHAPTER 31 LESSONS 3-4
(Student Page 301)

Guidelines for Writing Assignment #38: My Autobiography

An **autobiography** is the story of a person's life that is written by that person.
A **biography** is the story of a person's life that is written by someone else.

You will write an autobiography by telling about your life. An outline is provided below to help guide you.

I. Family
   A. Birth
   B. Parents
   C. Brothers and sisters
   D. Grandparents
   E. Most influential family member

II. Family life
   A. Chores and responsibilities
   B. How we celebrate special holidays
   C. Family vacations
   D. Special things about my family
   E. My goals and ambitions

III. School days
   A. Friends
   B. Teachers
   C. Best and worst subjects
   D. Special things about school
   E. My goals and ambitions

IV. Special interests
   A. Hobbies
   B. My achievements
   C. My likes and dislikes
   D. Other
   E. My goals and ambitions
   F. The other most influential person in my life

CHAPTER 31 LESSON 5
(Student Page 303)

Questions on *The Story of the Golden Bird*

1. What character in the story fulfills Element #1?
2. Name the three things (or persons) that have to be recovered or won by the hero.
3. Name the ordeal that the hero must go through (task he must perform) to win the hand of the Beautiful Princess.
4. Who (or what) fulfills Element #4?
5. A. What three warnings does the hero ignore when he must retrieve the three things or people?

    B. What two warnings does the hero ignore after he refuses to kill the fox?
6. Find an example of the use of repetition for effect in the story.
7. Explain:

    A. How the ending is happy.

    B. What villains die.